Finnish Air Force

1939 - 1945

**By Kalevi Keskinen
and Kari Stenman
Color by Don Greer**

Don Greer

squadron/signal publications

Kapteeni (Captain) Jorma Karhunen of the 3rd Flight, *Lentolaivue* 24, engages and destroys a Russian Pe-2 over Maaselkä in eastern Finland on 2 July 1942. Capt Karhunen was awarded the Mannerheim Cross in September of 1942 and in May of 1943, assumed command of LeLv 24. He ended the war with 31.5 kills after flying Fokker D.XXIs and Brewster B-239s.

ISBN 0-89747-387-6

If you have any photographs of aircraft, armor, soldiers or ships of any nation, particularly wartime snapshots, why not share them with us and help make Squadron/Signal's books all the more interesting and complete in the future. Any photograph sent to us will be copied and the original returned. The donor will be fully credited for any photos used. Please send them to:

Squadron/Signal Publications, Inc.
1115 Crowley Drive.
Carrollton, TX 75011-501010

Если у вас есть фотографии самолетов, вооружения, солдат или кораблей любой страны, особенно, снимки времён войны, поделитесь с нами и помогите сделать новые книги издательства Эскадрон/Сигнал ещё интереснее. Мы переснимем ваши фотографии и вернем оригиналы. Имена приславших снимки будут сопровождать все опубликованные фотографии. Пожалуйста, присылайте фотографии по адресу:

Squadron/Signal Publications, Inc.
1115 Crowley Drive.
Carrollton, TX 75011-501010

軍用機、装甲車両、兵士、軍艦などの写真を所持しておられる方はいらっしゃいませんか？どの国のものでも結構です。作戦中に撮影されたものが特に良いのです。Squadron/Signal社の出版する刊行物において、このような写真は内容を一層充実し、興味深くすることができます。当方にお送り頂いた写真は、複写の後お返しいたします。出版物中に写真を使用した場合は、必ず提供者のお名前を明記させて頂きます。お写真は下記にご送付ください。

Squadron/Signal Publications, Inc.
1115 Crowley Drive.
Carrollton, TX 75011-501010

Photo Credits

ECPA
Ilmavoimat (The Finnish Air Force)
Keski-Suomen Ilmailumuseo (The Finnish Air Force Museum)
Lentorykmentti 4:n kilta (Guild of LeR 4)
SA-Kuva (The Finnish Defense Forces)
Suomen Ilmailumuseo (The Finnish Aviation Museum
VL (State Aircraft Factory)
Private and Authors' Collections

Introduction

As a result of both the First World War and the Russian revolution, Finland declared its independence from Czarist Russia on 6 December 1917. Believing a Bolshevik uprising in Finland would bring the country back to the Soviet Union, the revolutionary government in Russia supported the declaration. However, Finland went through a short civil war in early 1918 with government troops, the "White Army," supported by a number of German units, fighting the insurgent "Red Army" supported by a number of Russian units. The fighting ended victoriously for the White Army in May of 1918. The Treaty of Dorpat, signed with the Russians in 1920, formally recognized Finland as a sovereign nation.

During the civil war, on 6 March 1918, the Swedish Count Eric von Rosen donated the first aircraft to the White Army, a French designed Morane-Saulnier Type L Parasol. The Rosen family emblem of good luck, a blue swastika, was painted on the wings. This marking became the national insignia carried on all aircraft of the Finnish Air Force. This blue swastika had nothing to do with the later Nazi swastika, which became official in Germany only after Adolf Hitler took power in 1933, some fifteen years after the introduction of the Finnish insignia.

Throughout the civil war the Finnish Air Force had only a handful of aircraft. Using types like the Parasol, the German designed Albatros B. II and D.F.W. C.V, and French built Nieuport 10s and 23s, the Finnish Air Force flew only some 70 missions, mainly scouting and aerial photography. However, the value of aircraft was quickly realized and the ground work was laid for the systematic development of an air force, albeit restricted for many years by a lack of funds.

After the collapse of Germany in 1918, France became the primary supplier of military aircraft to Finland. Finland purchased aircraft such as the Breguet 14 bomber, Caudron G.3 reconnaissance biplane, Gourdou-Leseurre 21 fighter, and Caudron C.60, and Morane-Saulnier 50 trainers. Finland's own aircraft industry began in 1922 when the first of 122 I.V.L. A.22 Hansa float planes (a license built Hansa Brandenburg W34) were built at the State Aircraft Factory.

During the late twenties and early thirties England became the major supplier of fighters to Finland, delivering Martinsyde Buzzards, Gloster Gamecocks and Bristol Bulldogs. Holland supplied Fokker C.V reconnaissance aircraft. German Junkers K. 43s were purchased for conversion to light bombers and Czech Aero A-11s, A-32s, and Letov S 218s

were acquired for use as trainers. The locally designed and built Sääski, Tuisku and Viima light aircraft along with a number of British de Havilland Moths served as primary trainers. The British Blackburn Ripon was built under license for maritime work. Major General J. F. Lundquist assumed command of the Finnish Air Force in 1932, a position in which he would remain until 1945.

The first five-year development plan for the air force was issued in 1937. The plan required four army co-operation squadrons of 13 aircraft each, three bomber squadrons with 9 aircraft each, three fighter squadrons with 27 aircraft each, and one maritime squadron with 13 aircraft. From 1937 to 1939, Finland acquired 34 Fokker C. X army co-operation biplanes, 42 Fokker D.XXI fighters from Holland, and 18 Bristol Blenheim Mk I twin engine bombers from England. Although additional aircraft purchases had commenced in 1936, by the beginning of the Second World War, many of the authorized units were either partially or completely unequipped.

The outbreak of the Second World War saw the Finnish Air Force divided into three flying regiments. *Lentorykmentti 1* (LeR 1) possessed four army co-operation squadrons, LeR 2 operated two fighter squadrons, and LeR 4 had two subordinate bomber squadrons. A detached squadron (*Erillinen Lentolaivue* - ErLLv) was retained for maritime work.

Only two army co-operation squadrons, *Lentolaivue 10* (LLv 10) and LLv 12, were fully equipped with the new Fokker C. X, while LLv 14 had both Fokker C. X and the older C.V, while LLv 16 had obsolescent Blackburn Ripons and Junkers K. 43s. One fighter squadron, LLv 24, was equipped with new Fokker D.XXI aircraft, while LLv 26 was equipped with out-of-date Bristol Bulldogs. The two bomber squadrons, LLv 44 and LLv 46, were equipped with British-built Bristol Blenheim Is. A third bomber squadron had yet to form. The detached squadron, Er.LLv, was still flying Blackburn Ripons.

Considering the times, Finland was ill-equipped to fight a major conflict with any of the warring powers. Nevertheless, Finland would soon find herself embroiled in the military and political intrigues of Germany and the USSR. Finland would fight a short war with Russia in 1939-1940 (**The Winter War**), fight another with Russia from 1941 to 1944 (**The Continuation War**), and finally engage the Germans in Lapland in 1944 and 1945 (**The Lapland War**). Finland would successfully extricate herself from the conflict only when the Red Army was poised on the borders of the German Reich.

The second Bristol Blenheim Mk I (BL-105) was assigned to Immola on 15 November 1937. The unit, originally designated *Lentoasema* 6 (L.As. 6 - Flying Station 6), became *Lentorykmentti* 4 (LeR 4 - Flying Regiment 4) six weeks later when the Finnish Air Force reorganized their units and bases. Finland bought 18 of these modern twin engine bombers from England. The Finnish national insignia was a Medium Blue swastika on a White disk which had been introduced in March of 1918 and had no relationship with the Nazi swastika introduced some 15 years later. (Ilmavoimat)

(Above) *Lentolaivue* 46 (LLv 46 - Flying Squadron 46) Blenheims line-up at Immola on 8 October 1938. This unit was the second of the two squadrons in LeR 4. The Blenheims were painted in the standard British colors of dark green over sky gray. (Ilmavoimat)

(Left) A Fokker C. X flies over the Viipuri area on 11 May 1939. FK-85 was one of the State Aircraft factory license built aircraft attached to LLv 10, the dive-bombing element in LeR 1. Finland purchased four aircraft from Holland. The State Aircraft Factory (*Valtion Lentokonetehdas* - VL) built another 30 machines under license by January 1939. (Ilmavoimat)

This Fokker D.XXI (FR-80) was one of seven fighters bought from Holland. Another 35 D.XXIs were manufactured under license by the State Aircraft Factory (VL) through August of 1939. Dutch-built machines had dark brown upper and silver doped lower surfaces. (VL)

(Above) Finland purchased ten Czechoslovakian Letov S218 primary trainers and license built a further 29 from 1930 to 1936. These orange painted Letovs of the *Ilmailukoulu* (Aviation School) are visiting the air show held at Lentoasema 5 based at Suur-Merijoki near Viipuri on 3 August 1935. (Ilmavoimat)

(Right) The VL Viima (Draught) primary trainer was designed by the State Aircraft Factory and, in addition to two prototypes, a total of 22 were built in 1937 - 39. The second prototype VI-2, painted overall orange, is on the factory field at Tampere during May of 1938. (VL)

(Right) One Fokker C. VE was purchased from Holland in 1927 followed by thirteen in 1934. FO-77, issued to LLv 14, is being refueled at Parola on 3 August 1938. Fokker built aircraft were painted dark brown on the upper surfaces with silver dope on the undersides. By the Second World War, the Fokker C. VE was obsolete for army co-operation duties. (Ilmavoimat)

The VL Pyry (Blizzard) was another State Aircraft Factory design and was used as an advanced trainer. The prototype (PY-1) is seen at the factory in Tampere during July of 1939. Forty aircraft were built during 1941. Finnish built aircraft were painted olive green with light gray lower surfaces. (VL)

(Above) Six Bristol Bulldog IVA fighters attached to LLv 26 paid a visit to L.As. 3 at Sortavala on 9 March 1936, three days after Finnish Air Force Day. Seventeen Bulldogs were purchased from England in 1934. LLv 26 used Bulldogs during the Winter War claiming six aerial victories. (Ilmavoimat)

(Above) A single Blackburn Ripon IIF was purchased from England. A further 25 were built by VL by October of 1934. Despite their obsolescence, they were used for harassment bombings during the Winter War. This Panther-engined example belonging to LLv 14 based at Suur-Merijoki gleams in the sun on 16 February 1939. (Ilmavoimat)

(Below) The Fokker C. X played the main army co-operation role during the Winter War. FK-97, attached to LLv 12, is parked at the regimental base at Suur-Merijoki on 18 January 1939. (Ilmavoimat)

A Blenheim I (BL-106) of LLv 46 was used for fixed ski tests at the State Aircraft Factory during the Spring of 1939. Several Blenheims were fitted with these skis during the Winter War, but they were disliked by the crews. Eventually all aircraft were changed back to wheels. (VL)

The Winter War 1939-1940

Germany and the Soviet Union signed a non-aggression pact in late August of 1939. The pact included a secret agreement dividing eastern and northern Europe into areas of German or Russian interest. Finland and the Baltic nations of Estonia, Latvia, and Lithuania (all previously dominated by Czarist Russia) were considered to be within the interests of the Soviet Union.

On 1 September 1939, Germany invaded Poland and rapidly overran the western parts of the country, with the Soviet Union moving into the eastern part of Poland on 17 September 1939. The Soviet government forced the Baltic nations to hand over military bases on the southern coast of the Gulf of Finland. The following month, Soviet troops and parts of the Red Banner Baltic Fleet were transferred to these bases. Finland had over 1,000 miles of border with the Soviet Union and in the south only the 60 mile wide Gulf of Finland separated the two countries. The Finnish military-political situation had changed dramatically in less than two months.

By October of 1939 Moscow demanded the large scale withdrawal of Finnish forces from the border and the insertion of Soviet troops onto Finnish territory, ostensibly to ensure the defense of Leningrad. The Finnish government resisted the Soviet demands until the end of November when the Soviet government suddenly broke off negotiations on the 28th. The Red Army attacked Finland on 30 November 1939. The Russo-Finnish **Winter War** had begun.

Soviet troops attacked along the entire border with some 20 divisions supported by 2800 aircraft. Their left flank was covered by 450 additional aircraft of the Baltic Fleet

All Fokker C. Xs were flown with skis during the four to five month long winters. FK-99 of LLv 12 is being refueled during gas alarm exercises on 23 February 1939 at Suur-Merijoki. Finnish-built aircraft were camouflaged in olive green over light gray. (Ilmavoimat)

air forces. The Finnish Army could barely muster nine divisions, while only 114 front-line Finnish Air Force aircraft were available for air operations. Most of the aircraft were obsolete. A David and Goliath situation had developed.

The Fokker D.XXI fighters of LLv 24 enjoyed notable success from the beginning, destroying twelve bombers on the second day of the war and another dozen on 19 December. The Blenheim bombers of LeR 4 were used only on long range reconnaissance missions while other units went over to night operations to avoid losses.

Despite the numerical superiority of the Russians, the Finns were able to halt all Russian advances through the course of December. The Finnish Army inflicted severe losses on the Red Army using the wooded terrain and superior tactics. The Russians, realizing the low training standards of their troops, began a training program at the front and built up their forces on the Karelian Isthmus to 50 divisions totaling one million men. The Red Air Force increased its operational tempo, often flying over 1000 sorties above the front on a single day.

On the political front, the League of Nations declared the USSR to be an aggressor and expelled the Soviet Union on 14 December 1939. This opened the door for League member nations to offer assistance to Finland. England and France provided the bulk of the support, however Italy and the United States also contributed. The Finnish Air Force received 30 British Gloster Gladiators and 22 Bristol Blenheims, 30 French Morane-Saulnier MS 406s, and 32 Italian Fiat G.50s. Forty-four Brewster B-239 fighters, an export variant of the U.S. Navy Brewster

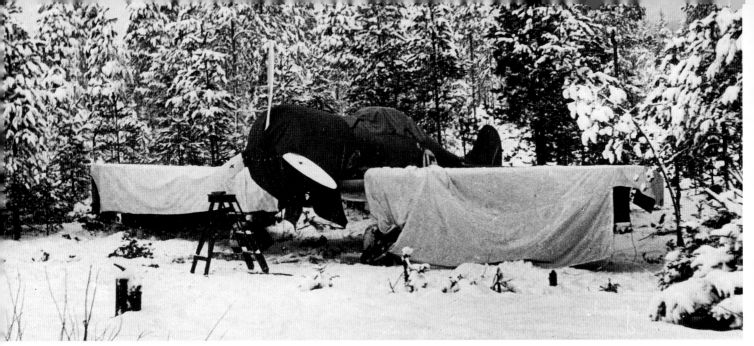

Fokker D.XXI (FR-86) of *Lentolaivue* 24 and wearing a coat of camouflage, was parked at Utti on 1 December 1939, the second day of the Winter War. The very same day, 2nd Flight leader *Luutnantti*

(Lieutenant) Jaakko Vuorela scored the squadron's first victory in this aircraft, when he shot down a Tupolev SB bomber. Skis were quickly fitted to all D.XXIs. (SA-kuva)

F2A Buffalo, were ordered from the US, but most of these did not arrive until after the winter conflict was over. Through the course of the Winter War, the Finns not only replaced all of their losses, but increased their front-line strength to 130 aircraft. Most of these aircraft were superior to the Polikarpov I-153 and I-16 fighters, Tupolev SB and Ilyushin DB-3 bombers, and Polikarpov R-5 reconnaissance aircraft operated by the Russians. With the additional resources, the bomber forces added another squadron — LLv 42 equipped with Blenheims — and could now switch to attacks in squadron strength. Greater numbers of higher quality fighters were now available to defend traffic junctions and supply depots in the rear.

The Winter War continued unabated into the new year. On 6 January 1940, Lt. Jorma Sarvanto, flying a Fokker D.XXI fighter, shot down six Soviet DB-3 bombers in four minutes as they returned from a mission in central Finland. The event received worldwide media attention and kept the Winter War in the forefront of the news.

Four days later, and despite official Swedish neutrality in the conflict,

the Swedish volunteer unit F 19 arrived in Lapland to counter Soviet bombing attacks. This regiment had a fighter squadron equipped with Gloster Gladiators and a light bomber flight possessing Hawker Harts. January also saw the addition of a new fighter squadron — LLv 28 equipped with French-built MS 406s.

The second phase of the Russian invasion began on 10 February 1940 and led to a temporary break-through in the Karelian Isthmus. By the end of the month however, the Finnish Army had stabilized the front between Viipuri (Vyborg) and Lake Ladoga and held these positions until the end of the hostilities. Finnish successes were not all one sided, however. On 29 February 1940, Soviet fighters flew deep into the rear and managed to surprise the Gladiators of LLv 26 at Ruokolahti air base. Three were shot down trying to take-off and two more were lost during the ensuing air combat.

On 4 March, the Soviet army attempted to cross the frozen Gulf of Finland west of Viipuri and all flying units were ordered to carry out ground attack missions against these troops. Concentrated low-level attacks caused considerable damage to the Soviet columns caught on the ice without shelter. Nevertheless, the Russians were able to turn the Finnish Army's flank and eventually secure the entire Karelian Isthmus.

Despite the stubborn opposition of the Finns and foreign political pressure on the Soviet government, the sheer weight of the Russian attacks made themselves felt. Furthermore, substantial foreign support was lacking. Britain and France were at war with Germany and other European nations were staying neutral. The United States, while sympathetic to the Finnish plight, had little desire to be involved in another European War.

Having little choice, Finland signed an armistice with Russia on 13 March 1940, handing over considerable territory along the border as a result. The Russians also occupied Hanko, a Finnish naval base at the entrance to the Gulf of Finland. The Russo-Finnish Winter War had lasted 105 days, during which the Finnish Air Force shot down 207 Russian aircraft with the anti-aircraft units claiming a further 314. Forty-eight Finnish aircraft were lost on operations while flying a total of 5,963 sorties — low when compared to the Red Air Force's 100,970 sorties on the Finnish front.

Finnish ace Lt Per-Erik Sovelius, deputy leader of the 4th Flight of LLv 24 (4/LLv 24) stands next to his Fokker D.XXI (FR-92) in January of 1940. Sovelius scored 5.75 victories flying D.XXIs in the Winter War and another seven flying Brewster B-239s in the Continuation War. The rudder of the plane has a white upper surface with a black tactical number. (Jorma Sarvanto)

(Above) FR-110, a Fokker D.XXI of 3/LLv 24, was flown exclusively by *Lentomestari* (Warrant Officer) Viktor Pyötsiä, who scored 7.5 victories during the Winter War. The fin carried 4.5 kill marks when it was damaged on 8 April 1940 at Joroinen after having lost the port ski in flight.

(Right) FR-99 was the mount of *Majuri* (Major) Gustaf Magnusson, the commander of LLv 24, and an ace with 5.5 victories in both wars. The aircraft is seen in January of 1940 with pilots of the 4th Flight. A black 1 was painted on the white rudder. (Jorma Sarvanto)

(Below) Blue 4 (FR-116) of 5/LLv 24 was parked at Joroinen on 8 April 1940. In less than two weeks the highly experienced LLv 24 would exchange their Fokker D.XXIs for Brewster Model 239s. Fokker D.XXI pilots ultimately downed 130 Soviet aircraft.

9

(Above) After the Russian onslaught, the French government donated 50 Morane-Saulnier MS 406 fighters to Finland. However, only 30 were received, all during February of 1940. MS306 was assigned to the 1st Flight of LLv 28 at Hollola. (Aarne Nissinen)

(Left) An Italian mechanic adjusts the Fiat A.74 engine of a Fiat G.50 fighter belonging to LLv 26 at Hollola on 13 March 1940. This was the last day of the Winter War. Finland bought 35 G.50 fighters from Italy. (SA-kuva)

(Below) White 6 (MS305) of 1/LLv 28 takes off for one of the last sorties of the Winter War from Hollola on 13 March 1940. Moranes scored 14 victories during the last weeks of the war. The aircraft wore the standard French three-color camouflage of khaki, earth, and dark blue-gray over light blue-gray under surfaces. (SA-kuva)

(Above) A Blenheim Mk IV (BL-129) of LLv 46 is refueled at Luonetjärvi on 7 March 1940 prior to a strafing mission in the Gulf of Viipuri. Twelve of these long nosed Blenheims were purchased from England in December of 1939. (SA-kuva)

(Right) Blenheim IV (BL-124) of LLv 46, has returned from a strafing mission on 8 March 1940. This batch of Blenheims was painted in the standard British colors of dark green over sky gray. The large building is the camouflaged main hanger of Luonetjärvi Air Base. (SA-kuva)

(Below) Sweden donated a single Douglas DC-2 to the Finnish Air Force. The aircraft is being prepared for its sole bombing sortie on 22 February 1940 at Joroinen. The aircraft bore the serial DC-1 and the inscription HANSSIN-JUKKA on the nose.

(Above) Finland purchased 20 Gloster Gladiator II fighters from England in December of 1939 and ten additional Gladiators were received as a gift. LLv 26 scored 34 victories flying the Gladiators during the Winter War. GL-270 of LLv 12 was based at Karhusjärvi ice base near Lappeenranta in March of 1940. (Ossi Marttila)

(Below) In 1939 Finland bought two Fieseler Fi 156K-1 Storch from Germany. ST-112 served as a hack for *Lentorykmentti* 1 and is seen parked at Kauhava in western Finland on 23 March 1940. (Ilmavoimat)

(Above) A winter-camouflaged Fokker C. VE (FO-68) served with *Lentolaivue* 14 in February 1940. Their primary missions were day-time reconnaissance and night harassment bombings of enemy camps. (Seppo Mäki)

(Below) Three British-built Avro Anson I aircraft were purchased in 1936 for bomber crew training. AN-101 of LeR 4 taxis for take off at Luonetjärvi on 7 March 1940. The Ansons were painted RAF Dark Green over Sky Gray. The cowlings were left natural metal. (SA-kuva)

The Winter War - Camouflage and Markings

Prior to the outbreak of World War II, Finnish Air Force (FAF) combat aircraft were painted in a simple scheme of olive green upper surfaces over light gray or silver dope lower surfaces. Aircraft purchased from other countries were usually left in their original color schemes until the aircraft went through a major overhaul. This practice was also applied to most advanced training aircraft, while basic training aircraft generally received an orange paint scheme for safety and visibility. A temporary white paint was sometimes used on upper surfaces during the winter for additional camouflage.

The FAF used a simple five digit alpha-numeric serial number. Two letters denoted the specific aircraft. Up to three numbers were used to indicate the serial within the aircraft type. Additionally, the number sequences did not necessarily correspond to the number of aircraft acquired or built within a series.

The FAF insignia was known as a *Hakaristi* (Broken Cross) or swastika. The insignia was usually applied to the fuselage sides and the top and bottom of both wings in medium blue on a white disk. The insignia had a specific orientation (horizontal and vertical arms) that was different from the German swastika. There were occasions when the FAF insignia was reversed. There was no fin flash.

A Swedish volunteer unit, *Flygflottilj* 19, arrived for the defense of Lapland on 10 January 1940. The unit consisted of twelve Gloster Gladiator II fighters and four Hawker Hart light bombers. The unit shot down eight Soviet aircraft and prevented the bombing of towns in Lapland. (Top) A Gladiator with a Yellow K on its rudder, warms up at Veitsiluoto near Kemi in January of 1940. (Center) A Hart, with a Black M on its rudder and over painted Finnish insignia, flies over Lapland in March of 1940 just before returning to Sweden. (Bottom) Six Gladiators of *Flygflottilj* 19 are lined up at Kauhava on 30 March 1940 prior to their departure for Sweden. Various emblems and kill markings were painted on the aircraft, although most seem to share a skull and crossbones. (Ilmavoimat)

The newly established LLv 32 received the Fokker D.XXIs of LLv 24 in April of 1940. Still wearing tactical numbers from the Winter War,

FR-92 and FR-95 have traded in their skis for wheels as they fly over western Finland during June of 1940.

The Truce 1940-1941

Many of the foreign aircraft purchased during the Winter War did not arrive until after the conflict ended. Included were a dozen British-built Westland Lysanders and Hawker Hurricanes, plus 44 US-built Brewster Model 239 fighters. The Brewsters would play a major part in the Finland's role in the conflagration about to engulf Europe.

In April of 1940, Germany invaded Denmark and Norway, occupying the former instantly and the latter by early June. Now sandwiched between Germany and the Soviet Union, Finland became geopolitically isolated from Western Europe. Since the hard terms of the truce were certainly not in favor of Finland, the Finnish government reluctantly sought assistance from Germany.

In June of 1940, Germany invaded Belgium, Holland and France while the Soviet Union swiftly occupied all of Estonia, Latvia and

Lithuania, although less violently. Finland had become even more isolated. During the fall of 1940, Germany began to offer a great deal of military assistance to the Finns and, unaware of German plans to invade Russia, the Finns accepted all the help they could get.

The Germans began selling captured war material from occupied countries to Finland. In 1940, the Finnish Air Force received ten Morane-Saulnier 406s. These were followed by another ten Moranes and 16 ex-French Curtiss Hawk 75As by the end of June 1941. The State Aircraft Factory, having obtained a production license in 1938, began production of Fokker D.XXIs. VL completed 50 during the first half of 1941. There was a price — by 8 June 1941, German troops were occupying areas of northern Finland for the coming invasion of Russia.

A Bristol Blenheim I (BL-136) of LLv 42, buzzes the control tower at Luonetjärvi in August of 1940. The unit was established during the Winter War with British pilots delivering the 12 aircraft on 26

February 1940. The aircraft wore the standard British night bomber scheme of dark green and dark earth over black under surfaces.

Twelve Hawker Hurricane Mk I fighters were purchased from England in February of 1940, however, two were lost enroute. The machines were placed in newly formed LLv 22, which did not see action in the Winter War. HU460 was seen at Helsinki-Malmi airport on 6 April 1940. The serial was changed to HC460 the following month. (Ilmavoimat)

In December of 1939, Finland bought 44 Brewster B-239 fighters from the United States, however, the planes arrived too late for the Winter War. BW-369 was on strength with LLv 22 on 6 April 1940. Two weeks later the Brewsters were handed over to LLv 24 and LLv 22 was disbanded. (Ilmavoimat)

A Fiat G.50 (FA-26) of *Lentolaivue* 26 paid a visit to Kauhava on 27 July 1940. During the Winter War, the Fiats were credited with 13 aerial victories. The camouflage is the Italian continental scheme consisting of a dark green mottle over medium brown upper surfaces and a light gray bottom. (Ilmavoimat)

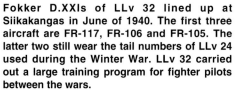

Fokker D.XXIs of LLv 32 lined up at Siikakangas in June of 1940. The first three aircraft are FR-117, FR-106 and FR-105. The latter two still wear the tail numbers of LLv 24 used during the Winter War. LLv 32 carried out a large training program for fighter pilots between the wars.

(Above) Pyry advanced trainers were painted like combat aircraft — olive green with black segments on the upper surfaces over light gray lower surfaces. PY-3 and PY-5 of LLv 34 are seen at Siikakangas in May of 1941. This advanced training squadron was disbanded on 1 October 1941. (Vilppu Lakio)

(Left) This Fokker D.XXI (FR-134) was powered by a Twin Wasp Junior and belonged to LLv 32 in May of 1941. The State Aircraft Factory built fifty Fokker D.XXIs powered by Twin Wasp engines during the first half of 1941. (Vilppu Lakio)

(Below) Finland captured eight Polikarpov I-153s during the Winter War, three more during the Continuation War, and bought an additional ten from Germany in 1942. The aircraft were used in the maritime reconnaissance role. VH-12 of LLv 6 was based at Turku on 13 June 1941. (Ilmavoimat)

(Above) Five Ilyushin DB-3M bombers were captured from the Russians during the Winter war and another six were purchased from Germany in 1941. VP-101 is at Luonetjärvi on 10 April 1940.

Lentolaivue 46 used the aircraft as a bomber crew trainer. The VP serials were changed to DB in September of 1941. (Finnish Air Force)

(Above) The State Aircraft Factory (VL) refurbished eight captured Tupolev SB bombers. A further 16 were purchased from Germany in 1941. This SB-2M103 (VP-10) was parked at the factory in Tampere during April of 1940. The prefix codes were changed to SB in September of 1941. (VL)

(Below) In March of 1941, Winter War veteran BL-106 received a new coat of war paint — olive green and black upper surfaces over light gray under surfaces. It was attached to LLv 44 at Siikakangas.

The Continuation War - 1941

The German plan to invade Russia (Operation Barbarossa) was kept secret from the Finnish government until the last minute. The German attack began during the early hours of 22 June 1941. Three days later the Red air force bombed several locations in Finland, which was still considered to be in a state of war with the Soviet Union. This Russian perception was reinforced by the presence of German forces in northern Finland attempting to cut off Murmansk and its vital port. Finland was now a reluctant comrade-in-arms with Germany.

The Finnish Air Force was now far better equipped to face the Russians. One fighter regiment, LeR 2 possessed 94 fighters in three squadrons, Brewsters in LeLv 24 (the Finns changed the abbreviation of *Lentolaivue* from *LLv* to *LeLv*), Fiat G.50s in LeLv 26 and MS 406s in LeLv 28. The other fighter regiment, LeR 3 had 61 fighters in two squadrons, both LeLv 30 and LeLv 32 being mainly equipped with Fokker D. XXIs. The latter soon received Curtiss Hawk 75As. The bomber regiment, LeR 4, consisted of 22 Blenheim bombers in three squadrons, LeLv 42, LeLv 44 and LeLv 46. Additionally, the tactical reconnaissance, army co-operation and maritime services had 58 aircraft in five independent squadrons bringing total front-line strength to 213 aircraft. The Soviet air forces were estimated to have 500 aircraft for use

The Finnish armed forces were mobilized on 17 June 1941, one week before the Continuation War began. All aircraft were given eastern front recognition markings consisting of yellow lower wing tips and a yellow rear fuselage band. The ground crew use a hand crank to start FR-125 of the 2nd Flight of *Lentolaivue* 30 (2/LeLv 30) at Hyvinkää in southern Finland on 11 July 1941. (SA-kuva)

along the Finnish front. The vast majority of their aircraft were now being concentrated against Germany.

On the first day, about 150 unescorted Soviet bombers appeared over southern Finland. In their first action, the Fiat G.50s of LeLv 26 shot down 13 bombers while the Brewsters of LeLv 24 scored another ten.

The Finnish Army finally joined the offensive against the Soviet Union on 10 July 1941, carrying out their attacks in three phases through the course of the summer. The first advance began north of Lake Ladoga, followed three weeks later by an attack into the Karelian Isthmus. On 4 September 1941, the Finns began a third drive to the River Svir, reaching it in four days. Simultaneously, the Germans arrived at the outskirts of Leningrad, putting the city under a siege that would last for 900 days.

In spite of German pressure, the C-in-C of the Finnish forces, Marshall C.G.E. Mannerheim, halted the Finnish attack toward Leningrad. Finnish forces continued farther north in order to recover land lost during the Winter War. When Finnish territory was recovered and favorable defensive positions were occupied by 6 December 1941, the Finns halted further offensive operations. The Finns then conducted a stationary defensive war that was to last for two and a half years.

Luutnantti Olli Puhakka of 3/LeLv 26 flew this Fiat G.50 coded FA-1. Puhakka was to score 42 victories and receive the Mannerheim Cross, the Finnish equivalent to the US Congressional Medal of

Honor. The pilots of LeLv 26 destroyed 13 Tupolev SB bombers in the first encounter on 25 June 1941. (SA-kuva)

This Brewster Model 239 (BW-372) was flown by the 2nd Flight leader of LeLv 24, *Kapteeni* Leo Ahola. His flight shot down ten Tupolev SB bombers on the first day of hostilities. Mechanics are working on the aircraft at Joensuu during July of 1941. (Esko Rinne)

During the Finnish advance, fierce air battles were fought by the fighters. Contrary to later western experience, the Brewster B-239 proved to be the ruler of the skies. In mid July B-239s destroyed 16 Russian planes and, together with other fighters, quickly gained aerial supremacy over Finnish spearheads. The Blenheim bombers meanwhile, successfully attacked Soviet supply lines and airfields in the Red Army's rear.

On 12 August 1941 the Brewsters of LeLv 24 shot down nine Russian I-153 biplane fighters on a single mission. The Fiats of LeLv 26 did the same the following day. On 3 September 1941, Curtiss Hawks of LeLv 32 flew the last combat over the advancing troops on the Karelian isthmus claiming seven fighters destroyed. Six days later the Moranes of LeLv 28 also shot down seven fighters over the River Svir.

The Brewsters were again in action east of Lake Onega on 23 and 26 September, shooting down seven and nine fighters respectively. Although numerous additional encounters occurred, no further major fighting took place. The bombers continued to harass the Kirov railway between Leningrad and Murmansk and were often assisted by the cannon-armed MS 406s in attacks on trains.

During the course of 1941 the Finnish Air Force had shot down 360 Soviet aircraft, while Finnish anti-aircraft artillery claimed another 103. Finnish operational losses amounted to 54 aircraft. Total Finnish front-line strength at the end of 1941 had dwindled to 110 aircraft.

The Continuation War — Camouflage and Markings

The beginning of the Continuation War saw the addition of German Luftwaffe style 'Eastern Front' markings to Finnish Air Force (FAF) aircraft. The markings consisted of a yellow aft fuselage band and lower wing tips. On 1 September 1941 fighters received a yellow cowling. During the Soviet's 'Great Offensive' in the summer of 1944, many FAF aircraft had the yellow paint on the upper cowling covered with camouflage paint.

The standard olive green and black camouflage with soft edges intro-

duced in November of 1940 was retained, however many Russian aircraft put into service by the FAF were given a hard edged splinter scheme of olive green and black.

The introduction of modern German aircraft — specifically Dornier Do 17Zs, Bf 109Gs, , and Junkers Ju 88As — into FAF service also introduced German paints. RLM 65 Hellblau (Light Blue-Gray), an undersurface color, had been adopted by the FAF for their own aircraft in May of 1942.

During the Continuation War, there were some efforts at toning down the national insignia by roughly overpainting the white disk with camouflage colors. In some cases, the white disk was deleted entirely leaving only a thin white edge around the blue swastika. Initially these efforts were carried out at the local level. A toned down national insignia, mandated by FAF regulations, was formally introduced in January of 1944 whereby the white disk was repainted with RLM 65 Hellblau.

Tactical numbers were usually painted on the rudders. Early Bf 109s, however, had their numbers painted on the engine cowling. Number colors could also be used to denote a flight. Tactical numbers could be one or more solid colors, or a simple outline. Colored spinners and rudders were also used to indicate flights within a squadron.

Kill markings were usually painted in white on the vertical stabilizer and/or rudder. Kill markings were generally in the form of a vertical bar or a silhouette of the destroyed aircraft.

Unit insignia were most often applied to the front fuselage, although there are numerous instances of their application to the aft fuselage or vertical stabilizer. Many of the unit insignia were very simplistic, using a contrasting camouflage color, white, and a stencil. Nose art, in the western Allies sense, was rare.

Warrant Officer Veikko Rimminen of 2/LeLv 24 taxis BW-367 to the runway at Rantasalmi in July of 1941. The flight colors consisted of a black spinner and rudder with a white number. LeR 2's three squadrons were tasked with maintaining air supremacy over the Finnish advance through Karelia. Rimminen scored five victories during the war. (Andreas Donner)

Ylikersantti (Staff Sergeant) Jalo Dahl of 4/LeLv 24 stands next to the nose of BW-393 at Rantasalmi in August of 1941. The spinner was red with a white stripe, while the rudder was white with a black number. These were the same markings used during the Winter War. The lower wing tips and aft fuselage band were yellow. (Jalo Dahl)

Seven ex-French Curtiss Hawk 75A-4s were purchased from Germany and LeLv 12 flew them for three weeks. CUc-502 is about to take off at Joroinen in July of 1941. The aircraft is flown by the future Mannerheim Cross holder and 1st Flight leader, Captain Auvo Maunula. (Jussi Laakso)

Vänrikki (2nd Lt) Martti Inehmo of 2/LeLv 28 flew this MS 406 coded MS-602 from Joroinen in July of 1941. This flight was identified by a red spinner and white tail number. LeLv 28 was one of LeR 2's three squadrons, the other two being LeLv 24 and LeLv 26. Inehmo scored a total of eight victories. (Pauli Massinen)

Kersantti (Sergeant) Sulo Suikkanen (sitting on the cockpit sill) and his ground crew pose in front of his Fiat G.50 (FA-15) at Rantasalmi on 28 June 1941. The 2nd Flight of *Lentolaivue* 26 had a yellow spinner and a black tail number bordered in yellow. The original Italian paints had a tendency to peel off. (Sulo Suikkanen)

(Above) BL-116 was a Blenheim of LeLv 44 stationed at Mikkeli on 31 July 1941. The following month the squadron would attack Soviet air bases on the Karelian Isthmus ahead of the Finnish advance. (SA-kuva)

(Right) The State Aircraft Factory built 15 short nosed Blenheim IIs under license in 1941. *Vääpeli* (Master Sergeant) Unto Oksala, a future Mannerheim Cross holder, stands in the cockpit of BL-149 of LeLv 44 at Onttola in October of 1941. (Lentorykmentti 4:n kilta)

(Below) BL-137, a Blenheim of LeLv 42, is about to take off from Joensuu on 21 August 1941. Missions were flown to Karelia in order to harass retreating Soviet troops. Russian I-16 fighters shot down this machine two weeks later. (SA-kuva)

Lentolaivue 16 was subordinate to the Karelian Army for army co-operation duties. The 1st Flight was equipped with Gladiators for close range reconnaissance. GL- 272 was still wearing the early British four-color camouflage of dark and light green and dark and light earth over black and white under surfaces on 1 July 1941. (SA-kuva)

LeLv 12 also supported the Karelian Army. The 3rd Flight was equipped with Fokker C. Xs for close support, aerial photography, and artillery fire control duties. FK-103 is rolled out for a sortie on 27 June 1941 at Mikkeli with flight leader Captain Ragnar Magnusson (wearing parachute) and his observer about to board the aircraft. (SA-kuva)

Twelve Westland Lysanders were purchased from England in 1940. 2/LeLv 16 flew them on reconnaissance and nuisance bombing missions throughout the Continuation War. LY-125, being gassed up at Joensuu in July of 1941, wears the standard British camouflage of dark green and dark earth over silver doped lower surfaces.

(Above) This Fokker D.XXI (FR-157) was flown by *Majuri* (Major) Lauri Bremer, the commander of LeLv 30. The aircraft is parked at Utti in September of 1941. The rudder has his personal emblem, the Ace of Hearts, and one victory bar. The spinner was red. (Lauri Bremer)

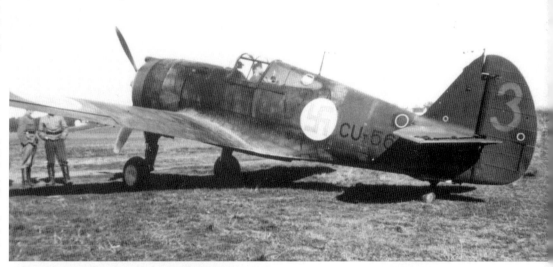

(Right) Finland purchased 22 Twin Wasp powered Hawk 75As from Germany in 1940. They were used by LeLv 32 until the end of the hostilities. Yellow 3 (CUw-563) is parked at Lappeenranta in September of 1941 wearing a patchy coat of Luftwaffe RLM 71 Dark Green over RLM 65 Blue-Gray. The white rings denote patched bullet holes. (Juhani Väisänen)

(Right) The Hurricanes flew primarily with LeLv 32 during the Continuation War, although a lack of spares kept many on the ground. HC 452's engine is being revved up at Lappeenranta in September of 1941. The yellow nose was painted on single-engined aircraft on the first day of September. The rudder has a black number with a white border. (Lauri Suominen)

(Above) White 4 (MS314) was an MS 406 flown by Lt Pauli Massinen (5 victories), the deputy flight leader of 2/LeLv 28. The aircraft is parked at a landing strip on the shore of Lake Ladoga in September of 1941. (Pauli Massinen)

(Below) Yellow 3 (FA-6), a Fiat G.50 of 3/LeLv 26, which was also based near Lake Ladoga in September of 1941. The regular pilot was Master Sergeant Onni Paronen, an ace with a total of 12.5 victories. The aircraft still wears the Italian camouflage and a row of victory marks on the bottom of the rudder. (Kauko Tuomikoski)

(Below) LeLv 10 existed for two months and flew reconnaissance missions in Fokker D.XXIs in South Viena. FR-144 was the mount of the 1st Flight leader Captain Pekka Käär and is crudely camouflaged with cut trees stuck in the ground at Tiiksjärvi on 4 October 1941. The yellow letter A indicated the flight leader. (SA-kuva)

The Winter War: November 1939 - March 1940

Fokker C. X dive bomber (FK-81) of 2/LLv 10 was stationed at Lappeenranta in December of 1939. Unlike other C. Xs, the Dutch-built machines were painted overall dark brown over silver dope under surfaces.

Fokker D.XXI fighter (FR-97) flown by Lt Jorma Sarvanto (17 victories) of 4/LLv 24 based at Immola in December 1939. In this aircraft on 6 January 1940, Lt Sarvanto shot down six Ilyushin DB-3M bombers in four minutes.

Bristol Blenheim I bomber (BL-117) flown by W/O Viljo Salminen of 1/LLv 44 based at Joroinen in February of 1940. The '21' on the rudder represents the number of bombing sorties flown by Salminen.

Morane-Saulnier MS 406 fighter (MS318) of 2/LLv 28 operating from Säkylä ice base in south-western Finland in February of 1940. The camouflage is the standard French three-color scheme of khaki green, earth and dark blue-gray over light blue-gray. A single white victory star as on the port side of the vertical fin, while on the starboard side, it was on the rudder.

Gloster Gladiator I fighter of the Swedish volunteer unit F 19 based at Veitsiluoto. 2nd Lt Ian Iacobi scored the unit's first victory, a Polikarpov I-15bis, in this aircraft on 12 January 1940.

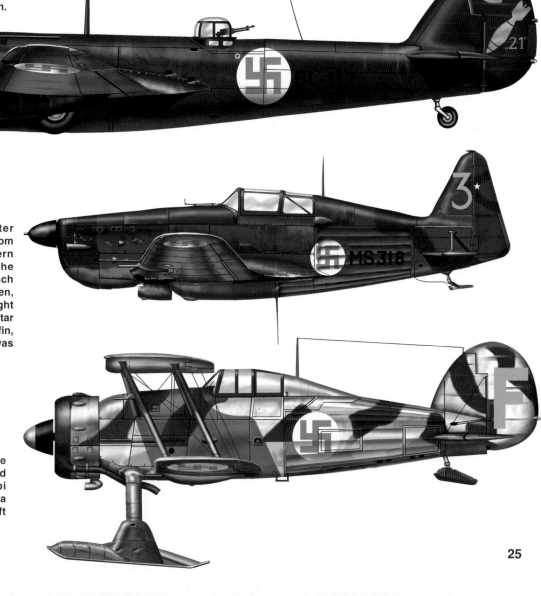

(Left) A Brewster B-239 (BW-379) of 3/LeLv 24, lands at Immola in September of 1941. Lt Pekka Kokko, an ace with 13.33 victories, was the regular pilot and acted as the deputy leader of the 3rd Flight. The flight color orange was used to paint the spinner and rudder number. (SA-kuva)

(Left) *Vääpeli* Lasse Heikinaro of 4/LeLv 24 prepares for take off in BW-394 at Immola in September of 1941. *Lentolaivue* 24 had a leaping lynx as the squadron emblem. The white edge around the lynx shaped stencil was painted by hand and each edging was slightly different in shape. (SA-kuva)

(Below) BW-353 belonged to 3/LeLv 24 and was the personal aircraft of Sergeant Jussi Huotari, a 17.5 victory ace. The aircraft is parked on a shore landing strip of Lake Ladoga in September of 1941. (Jouko Timonen)

(Right) Warrant Officer Oiva Tuominen of 1/LeLv 26 is sitting on the tail of his Fiat G.50 (FA-26) at Lunkula on 13 August 1941. Four days later he became the first Mannerheim Cross holder in the Finnish Air Force after gaining 20 victories. Tuominen ended the war with 44 victories — eight of them scored during the Winter War. (Oiva Tuominen)

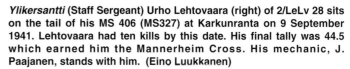

(Right) *Lentomestari* Ilmari Juutilainen of 3/LeLv 24 poses in front of his weathered Brewster (BW-364) at Hirvas shortly after receiving the Mannerheim Cross on 26 April 1942. On 28 June 1944 he became one of only four Finnish soldiers to receive the Mannerheim Cross for the second time. Juutilainen went on to become the top scoring Finnish fighter pilot with 94 confirmed victories.

A relaxed Sgt Nils Katajainen of 3/LeLv 24 sits on the tail of his Brewster (BW-368) at Mantsi on 26 September 1941 after his sixth kill. He would eventually gain 35.5 victories and the Mannerheim Cross. (Nils Katajainen)

Ylikersantti (Staff Sergeant) Urho Lehtovaara (right) of 2/LeLv 28 sits on the tail of his MS 406 (MS327) at Karkunranta on 9 September 1941. Lehtovaara had ten kills by this date. His final tally was 44.5 which earned him the Mannerheim Cross. His mechanic, J. Paajanen, stands with him. (Eino Luukkanen)

The Continuation War: June 1941 - September 1944

Curtiss Hawk 75A-4 fighter (CUc-502) was flown by Capt Auvo Maunula while commanding 1/LeLv 12 and based at Joensuu in July of 1941. The Hawks in his flight carried the face of "Stalin The Devil". Maunula received the Mannerheim Cross in 1942.

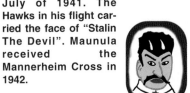

Fokker D.XXI (FR-119) flown by Lt Teuvo Ruohola of 2/LeLv 30 based at Suulajärvi on the Karelian Isthmus in November of 1941. This unit was very effective against Soviet light surface vessels.

Fiat G.50 (FA-26), flown by W/O Oiva Tuominen (44 victories) of 1/LeLv 26 based on a shore landing strip of Lake Ladoga at Lunkula in September of 1941. Tuominen became the first Mannerheim Cross holder in the Finnish Air Force on 18 August 1941.

Brewster Model 239 (BW-378) was the mount of Lt Per-Erik Sovelius (13 victories) while leading 4/LeLv 24. The flight was based on a shore landing strip of Lake Ladoga at Lunkula in October of 1941. The inscription OTTO WREDE was painted in honor of the donor — the Hamilton family in Sweden.

Under surfaces are painted silver

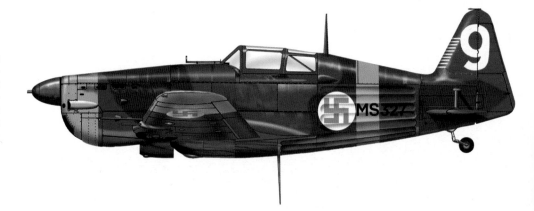

Morane 406 (MS327) issued to MSgt Urho Lehtovaara (44.5 victories) of 2/LeLv 28. The aircraft was based at Viitana on the western shore of Lake Onega in November of 1941. Lehtovaara won the Mannerheim Cross in

This Hawker Hurricane I (HC-456) was issued to Capt Heikki Kalaja, commander of 1/LeLv 30 while based at Utti in July of 1941. Kalaja's initials were painted below the cockpit. The camouflage is standard British dark green and dark earth upper surfaces with black, white, and silver lower surfaces.

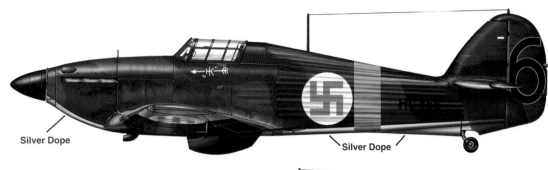

Silver Dope

Silver Dope

Fokker D.XXI (FR-148) was flown by Lt Martti Kalima (10.5 victories) of 3/LeLv 30. Kalima was stationed at Tiiksjärvi in Russian Karelia during June of 1942. He chose the Pinocchio for his emblem.

Fokker C.X light bomber (FK-97) was assigned to 3/LeLv 16. It was based at Viiksjärvi village on the ice of Lake Onega in March of 1942.

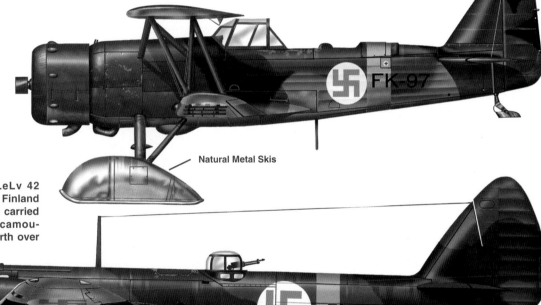

Natural Metal Skis

A Blenheim I (BL-136) of 2/LeLv 42 based at Luonetjärvi in central Finland in July of 1941. The Blenheims carried the standard British bomber camouflage of dark green and dark earth over black for night operations.

This Brewster 239 (BW-376) was piloted by W/O Viktor Pyötsiä (19.5 victories) of 1/LeLv 24 and based on the Olonets Isthmus at Nurmoila in October of 1941. The squadron emblem, a "Spitting Lynx", was outlined in white on a camouflage background.

The Continuation War 1942 - 1943

Fortunately, the now stabilized front gave little reason for major air operations. Both sides continued patrolling, however, resulting in local fighter engagements along the front during the first three months. In late March of 1942, the Finns assembled a 60 plane force to cover the seizure of the strategically important island of Suursaari (Gogland) in the central Gulf of Finland. The operation was successful with the island being occupied on 28 March 1942. While flying top cover for the occupation force, twelve Curtiss Hawk 75s of LeLv 32 engaged 29 Russian fighters shooting down fifteen, without loss to themselves.

Lend-lease aircraft sent to the Soviet Union began to arrive by ship at the Arctic Sea port of Murmansk during December of 1941. The aircraft were then flown south to the Leningrad area. A flight of Brewsters was sent to southern Viena (west of the White Sea) to interdict the flights. A number of successful engagements were fought with the Brewsters shooting down eight Russian Hurricanes on 30 March 1942, and claiming another eleven fighters and a bomber one week later.

During the second week of April, the Soviets attempted to breach the Finnish lines on the River Svir, but were halted by a Finnish counter attack. These successes were not all one-sided, however, since the bomber regiment supporting the counter attack with night missions lost three Blenheims when they exploded over the target due to faulty securing pins on the bombs.

On 3 May 1942, a major re-organization took place in the air force. Finnish air regiments were given territorial responsibility from the White Sea to the Gulf of Finland, while the Germans covered the northern half of the country.

LeR 1 took charge of the Olontets Isthmus with two squadrons, LeLv 32 flying Curtiss Hawk 75 fighters and LeLv 12 using Fokker D.XXIs and Fokker C. Xs for reconnaissance and army co-operation missions.

LeR 2 covered the Lake Onega sector with three squadrons. LeLv 24 with Brewster B-239s. LeLv 28 was equipped with MS 406 fighters (30 more had been purchased from unoccupied Vichy France.) LeLv 16 flew Gladiators, Lysanders and Fokker C. Xs for tactical reconnaissance and army co-operation duties.

LeR 3 was on the Karelian Isthmus with two fighter squadrons, LeLv 26 with Fiat G.50s and LeLv 30 flying Fokker D.XXIs.

LeR 4, the bomber regiment with four squadrons, was used where necessary. LeLv 42 and LeLv 44 were equipped with Blenheims, LeLv 46 was flying Dornier Do 17Zs that had recently arrived from Germany, and LeLv 48 was to receive captured Russian DB-3s and Pe-2s.

Two independent squadrons were in charge of both flanks. LeLv 14 flew Fokker D.XXIs reinforced with Brewsters and Fokker C. Vs in southern Viena. LeLv 6 flew anti-submarine missions with captured Tupolev SBs over the Gulf of Finland.

By the mid-summer of 1942, the war in the East was moving into its second year and Finnish hopes for a quick German victory over Soviet Russia were fading. Due to increased Soviet Baltic Fleet air force activity, on 1 August 1942, it was necessary to transfer a major part of LeLv 24 to the Karelian Isthmus under the control of LeR 3. Fierce air battles began on 12 August 1942 and, during the first week, the Russians lost 39 fighters for the cost of one Brewster B-239. The aerial combat continued unabated into September when six Curtiss Hawk 75s of LeLv 32 engaged a 40-plane Russian fighter regiment over the River Svir. Thirteen Soviet aircraft of various types were shot down without loss.

By the late fall of 1942 the Finns had received enough captured Russian aircraft from their own and German efforts to form a fifth regiment. Formed on 5 November 1942, LeR 5 was equipped with two squadrons for maritime duties. LeLv 6 flew captured Tupolev SBs along

This camouflaged and snow covered Brewster (BW-388) belonged to the 3/LeLv 24 and was flown by the deputy leader Lt Osmo Kauppinen, an ace with 5.5 victories. The unit was based on the ice of Kontupohja harbor on 15 February 1942. The number on the rudder was orange. (SA-kuva)

with various obsolete float planes, while LeLv 30 received Polikarpov I-153 fighters.

In contrast to the air battles of the summer and fall, the year ended quietly. During the course of 1942, Finnish fighters had shot down 355 Soviet aircraft with anti-aircraft artillery claiming another 103. Finnish combat losses totaled 34 aircraft, leaving 135 aircraft on strength on 31 December 1942.

The war in Europe was now slowly turning to the advantage of the Allies. The Finnish front was stalled and the German Army had been stopped short of capturing Leningrad or Moscow. German armies were being encircled at Stalingrad and retreating across North Africa. The Germans realized it would be useful to keep and arm as many friends as possible. After two years of persistent Finnish efforts, Germany agreed to sell modern German aircraft to Finland. During March of 1943 a new fighter squadron, LeLv 34, was added to LeR 3 and equipped with 30 new Messerschmitt Bf 109G-2 fighters.

The next month saw the arrival of 23 Junkers Ju 88A-4 bombers for LeLv 44, which passed its remaining Blenheims on to LeLv 42. LeLv 42 had faced a serious set-back on 19 February 1943 when three of its bombers were lost and five damaged on a mission during a snow-storm.

The qualitative superiority that the new German aircraft provided was short lived. During the spring of 1943, the Soviet Baltic Fleet air forces were re-equipped with Yakovlev Yak-7 and Lavochkin La-5 fighters, Ilyushin Il-2 attack aircraft, and Petlyakov Pe-2 and Douglas Boston bombers. The new Soviet aircraft were used to attack Axis supply vessels (Finland was an important source of nickel ore) and points of the mine belt across the Gulf of Finland. The mine belt was effectively bottling up Soviet ships to the east.

The Brewsters of LeLv 24 faced the challenge of newer Soviet aircraft with this obsolescent fighter once again showing its mettle, claiming 19

aircraft shot down on 18 April 1943 and another 17 three days later. The successes continued through the next month. During a six week period, the Brewster pilots sent 81 Russian aircraft into the sea for the loss of only two of their own. During the same period, the Bf 109s of LeLv 34 destroyed 46 more aircraft, making it a very costly period for the Red Banner Baltic Fleet air forces.

After a quiet period, the Soviet Union began an August aerial offensive that caused considerable damage to the Finnish supply lines and the mine-belt. On 17 September the bomber regiment countered with a bombing attack against a major Russian air base on the island of Lavansaari in the Gulf of Finland. Increasing mist and low clouds prevented accurate bombing. Two bombers were lost and seven more damaged on the return flight.

The fighting in the air continued with small groups of Finnish fighters often engaging much larger formations of Russian aircraft. On 23 September 1943 four Brewster B-239s and four Messerschmitt Bf 109s returning from a mission to the German front, engaged a formation of 20 Soviet fighters over the eastern Gulf of Finland. Fifteen Russian fighters were shot down without loss to the Finns.

During the fall of 1943 LeLv 48 was given 30 new Blenheims assembled by the State Aircraft Factory. This brought the bomber regiment up to its full strength of four squadrons that were now flying a mix of Blenheims, Ju 88s, Do 17s as well as a few Russian aircraft.

By the year's end Finnish fighters had shot down 307 Russian aircraft for the loss of 35 of their own aircraft. The ground defense forces claimed only 16, which reflects the lack of activity in the ground war on the Finnish Front. At the end of the year, the serviceable strength of the Finnish Air Force had risen to 188 aircraft.

Finland purchased 25 Morane fighters, including ten MS 410s mounting four wing guns, from Germany in 1940. MS-607 was one of the MS 410s and is seen at Viitana on 17 March 1942. It was flown by 2nd Lt Aarre Linnamaa, a six victory ace with 1/LeLv 28. The black tail number was edged with white. (SA-kuva)

This Lysander (LY-118) underwent a major repair at the State Aircraft Factory at Tampere in March of 1942. Skis were specially designed for the Lysander and were used during all winter operations. (Aaretti Nieminen)

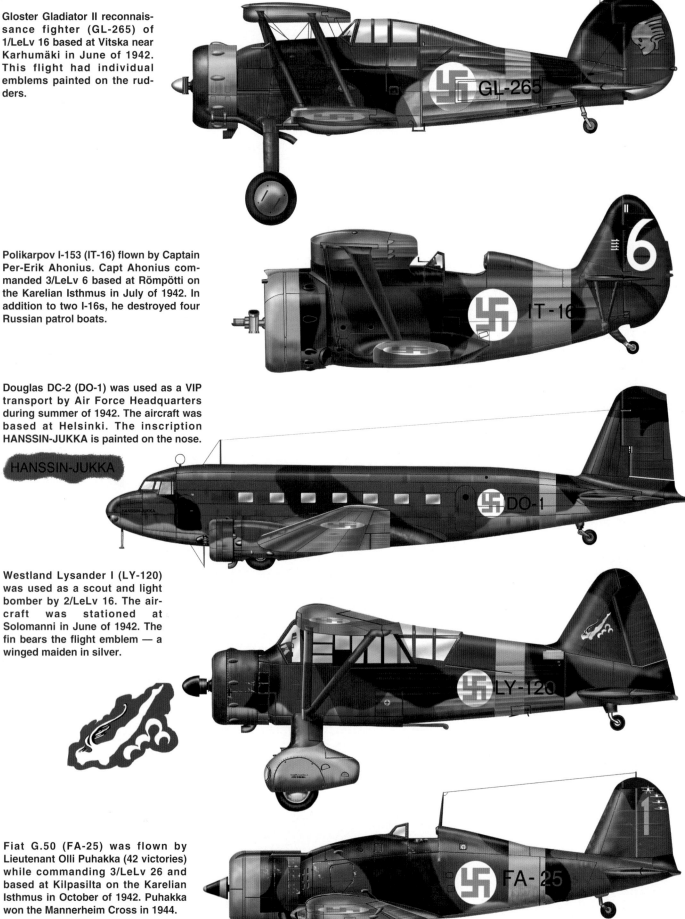

Gloster Gladiator II reconnaissance fighter (GL-265) of 1/LeLv 16 based at Vitska near Karhumäki in June of 1942. This flight had individual emblems painted on the rudders.

Polikarpov I-153 (IT-16) flown by Captain Per-Erik Ahonius. Capt Ahonius commanded 3/LeLv 6 based at Römpötti on the Karelian Isthmus in July of 1942. In addition to two I-16s, he destroyed four Russian patrol boats.

Douglas DC-2 (DO-1) was used as a VIP transport by Air Force Headquarters during summer of 1942. The aircraft was based at Helsinki. The inscription HANSSIN-JUKKA is painted on the nose.

HANSSIN-JUKKA

Westland Lysander I (LY-120) was used as a scout and light bomber by 2/LeLv 16. The aircraft was stationed at Solomanni in June of 1942. The fin bears the flight emblem — a winged maiden in silver.

Fiat G.50 (FA-25) was flown by Lieutenant Olli Puhakka (42 victories) while commanding 3/LeLv 26 and based at Kilpasilta on the Karelian Isthmus in October of 1942. Puhakka won the Mannerheim Cross in 1944.

Brewster 239 (BW-393) was flown by 3/LeLv 24 commander Lt Hans Wind (75 victories) in September of 1943 while based at Suulajärvi on the Karelian Isthmus. The fin would eventually carry all of his 39 kills scored while flying Brewsters.

Morane 406 (MS-311) was piloted by 2nd Lt Lasse Kurten of 1/LeLv 14 while based at Tiiksjärvi in July of 1943. This was the only known use of a large shark-mouth marking on Finnish aircraft.

This Messerschmitt Bf 109G-2 (MT-214), was the mount of SSgt Lauri Jutila (7.5 victories) of 2/LeLv 34 in June of 1943. The camouflage was the standard German grays of RLM 74/75 over RLM 76.

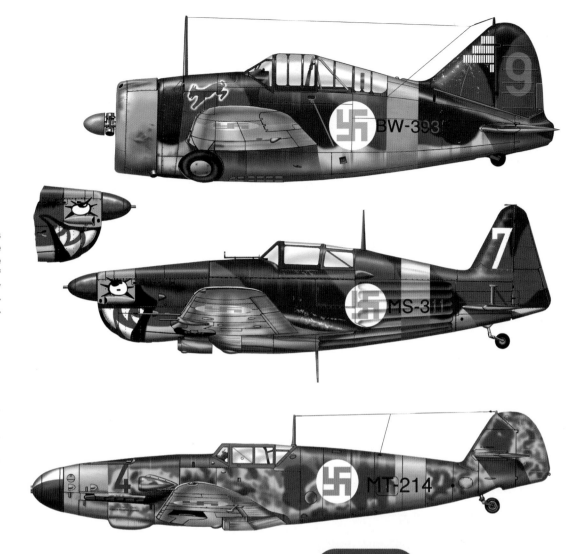

Tupolev SB-2M103 (SB-1) was flown by Lt Erkki Forsten of 2/LeLv 6 in the anti-submarine role. The aircraft was based at Helsinki-Malmi in October of 1942. The flight emblem and four submarine kill markings are painted on the tail.

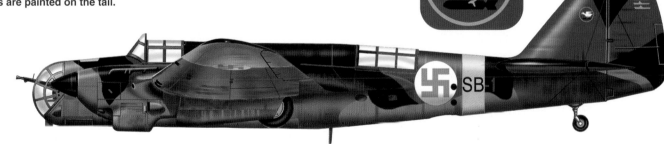

Dornier Do 17Z-3 (DN-64) issued to W/O Viljo Salminen of the Mapping Flight of LLv 48 based at Onttola in April of 1943. The tail shows 21 mapping sorties and the farting moose of 2/LLv 24. In 1941 Salminen was awarded the Mannerheim Cross.

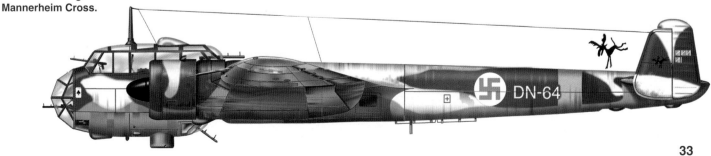

(Above) Blenheims IIs of LeLv 42 flew from Värtsilä in February of 1942. BL-159 still has its wheels, while BL-160 has been fitted with retractable skis designed by the factory. These skis saw limited use during the winters of 1942/43 and 1943/44. (ECPA)

(Left) By February of 1942, the only remaining long nosed Blenheim (BL-129) belonged to *Lentolaivue* 44 at Luonetjärvi. It was flown on mapping missions by the 1st Flight leader Captain Erkki Ahtiainen. (Ilmavoimat)

(Left) The Danish Red Cross donated a single Fokker F.VIIa passenger aircraft to Finland in 1941. During the invasion of Suursaari, it flew ambulance missions with LeLv 6. Later, it ferried guerrillas behind the lines while assigned to LeLv 16. FE-2 has just returned from a mission at Immola on 23 April 1942. (Pauli Ervi)

(Above) A Dornier Do 17Z-3 (DN-54) awaits her crew at Luonetjärvi in April of 1942. The aircraft, assigned to LeLv 46, used a tossing bull on a white shield as a squadron emblem.

(Right) A Dornier Do 17Z-3 (DN-55) is parked on the ice at Linnunlahti near Joensuu in April of 1942. It was a common practice to use a white-wash paint for the winter camouflage.

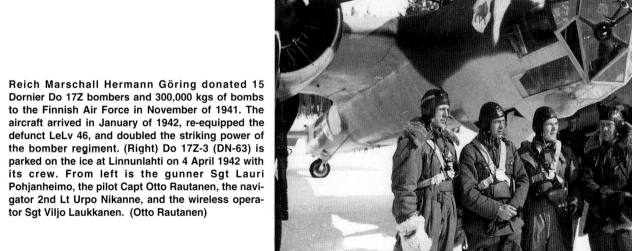

Reich Marschall Hermann Göring donated 15 Dornier Do 17Z bombers and 300,000 kgs of bombs to the Finnish Air Force in November of 1941. The aircraft arrived in January of 1942, re-equipped the defunct LeLv 46, and doubled the striking power of the bomber regiment. (Right) Do 17Z-3 (DN-63) is parked on the ice at Linnunlahti on 4 April 1942 with its crew. From left is the gunner Sgt Lauri Pohjanheimo, the pilot Capt Otto Rautanen, the navigator 2nd Lt Urpo Nikanne, and the wireless operator Sgt Viljo Laukkanen. (Otto Rautanen)

Curtiss Hawk 75A-3 (CU-582) of HLeLv 32 was based at Nurmoila on Olonets Isthmus in May of 1944. The Hawks were not allocated to individual flights. The white bar marked various detachments.

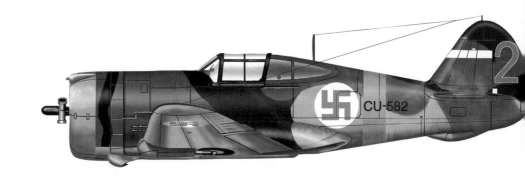

Curtiss P-40M-1-CU Warhawk (KH-51) of HLeLv 32 was based at Mensuvaara in Karelia in July of 1944. The machine was thought to be a Kittyhawk, hence the KH serial.

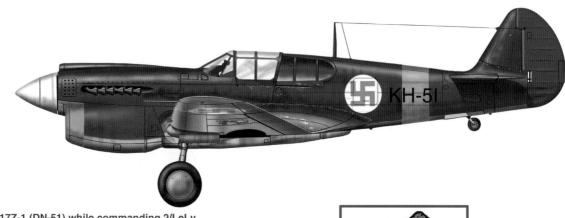

Capt Jussi Räty flew Do 17Z-1 (DN-51) while commanding 2/LeLv 48 at Immola in June of 1943. The squadron used a tossing bull as a unit emblem. The lower surfaces, normally painted RLM 65 Hellblau, were painted in silver dope on this aircraft.

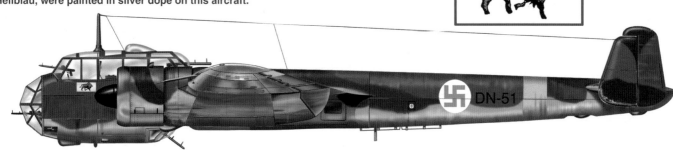

Bf 109G-2 (MT-213) was flown by Lt Eero Riihikallio (16 victories) of 2/HLeLv 24. Riihikallio was based at Suulajärvi on the Karelian Isthmus in May of 1944. The number 3 on the nose belongs to the aircraft's previous unit, 1/HLeLv 34.

Lavochkin LaGG-3 (LG-1) of LeLv 32 was stationed at Nurmoila on the Olonets Isthmus in September of 1943. The splinter type of camouflage was only applied to captured aircraft.

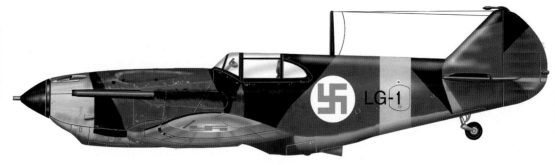

Bf 109G-6/R6 (MT-451) interceptor was flown by SSgt Erik Lyly (8 victories) of 1/HLeLv 34 while based at Taipalsaari in July of 1944. The fledgling eagle emblem had become the official squadron badge during the previous month.

Curtiss Hawk 75A-2 (CU-574) of HLeLv 32 was stationed at Nurmoila on the Olonets Isthmus in February of 1944. The two white bars on the fin denote a detached unit.

Bristol Blenheim IV (BL-201) was piloted by Maj Erkki Ahtiainen while commanding PLeLv 48 at Onttola in August of 1944. The squadron badge was a devil riding on a bomb while the tactical marking was a large letter 'A' on the rudder.

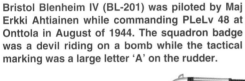

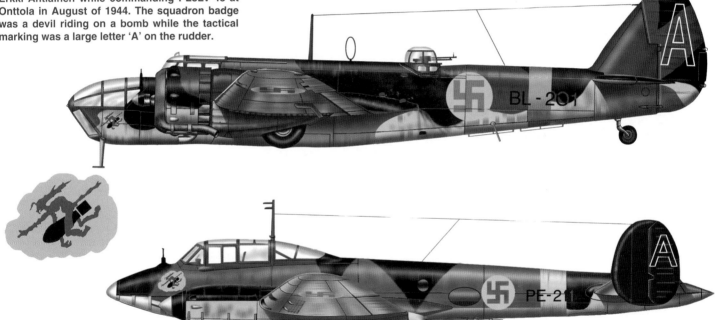

(Above) Petlyakov Pe-2 (PE-211) photo reconnaissance aircraft was issued to Capt Jaakko Ranta when he led 2/PLeLv 48 at Onttola in August of 1944. Both forms of squadron identification were applied.

(Below) Junkers Ju 88A-4 (JK-256) was flown by Capt Erkki Itävuori, the commander of 1/PLeLv 44 at Onttola in June of 1944. The laughing face was the flight emblem.

LeLv 12 used the well worn Mercury-powered Fokker D.XXIs for short range reconnaissance on the Olonets Isthmus. FR-95 of the 2nd Flight is warming up for take off at Nurmoila in April of 1942. The unit emblem was a white jumping donkey. (Erkki Havola)

White 1 (BW-358) rests on retractable skis at Tiiksjärvi in January of 1942. The 2nd Flight of *Lentolaivue* 24 was to stay there almost the whole year, tasked with stopping the flow of Lend-Lease aircraft from Murmansk to the south.

(Below) 2/LeLv 24 pilot SSgt Heimo Lampi flew BW-354 with a stylized white 6 on it's rudder. The aircraft is parked at Tiiksjärvi in April of 1942. The Brewsters were very successful against Soviet Hurricanes and in two months shot down 40 of them. Lampi ended the war with 13.5 victories. (Kaarlo Temmes)

(Above) BL-111 of LeLv 44 paid a visit to Tiiksjärvi in October of 1942. This Blenheim was usually flown by *Luutnantti* Sakari Heiskanen, deputy leader of the 3rd Flight. (Pauli Ervi)

(Right) Three ex-French Hanriot H.232.2 trainers were purchased from Germany in 1941. HT-193, assigned to *Täydennyslentolaivue* 17 (T-LeLv 17) was used for advanced training at Karvia in western Finland in September of 1941.

(Below) A Do 17Z-3 (DN-58) of *Lentolaivue* 46 sits on the field at Nurmoila on 10 June 1942. The Dorniers introduced RLM 65, a light blue-gray under surface color, which was adopted by the Finnish Air Force from May of 1942. The color was applied to aircraft as re-painting was necessary. (Ilmavoimat)

Ju 88A-4 (JK-268) was flown by W/O Unto Oksala of 3/PLeLv 44 and based at Onttola in June of 1944. Oksala had received the Mannerheim Cross the previous year.

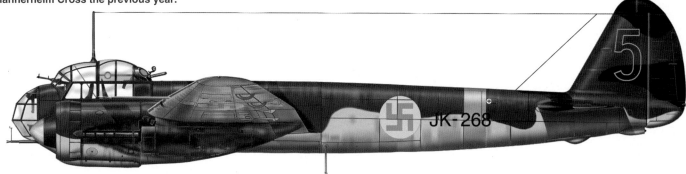

Brewster 239 (BW-368) belonged to 2/HLeLv 26 at Immola in June of 1944. New regulations placed the second flight tactical number below or behind the cockpit in Lentorykmentti 3 and 5 fighter squadrons.

This Morane 406 (MSv-631) was flown by SSgt Lars Hattinen (6 victories) of 1/HLeLv 28 while based at Värtsilä in August of 1944. MS 406 fighters were known as Mörkö Moranes after they were re-engined with captured Russian 1100 hp Klimov M-105 powerplants.

VL Myrsky II (MY-22) of HLeLv 26 was based at Kemi in October of 1944. The white lightning bolt on the cowling belonged to 2/TLeLv 12, the aircraft's previous unit. Fresh olive green paint covered the yellow eastern front markings on the cowl and aft fuselage.

Ilyushin DB-3M bomber (DB-13) of PLeLv 46 based in Kemi in October of 1944. The yellow eastern front band on the aft fuselage was covered with fresh olive green paint. The nose and fin markings were a carry over from the Mapping Flight of PLeLv 48.

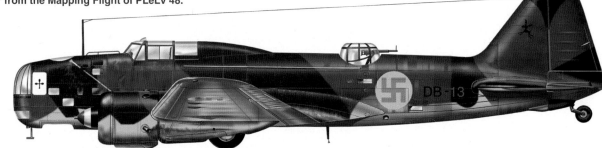

(Above) This Curtiss Hawk (CU-558) of Lentolaivue 32 is at Nurmoila on 2 August 1942. These aircraft were not distributed to the flights. The tail number (White 8) was the last number of the serial. *Kersantti* Niilo Erkinheimo was the top scoring pilot in CU-558 with 10.75 victories. (Ilmavoimat)

(Right) Gladiator (GL-270) flew with 1/LeLv 16 and is seen at Solomanni near Petrozavodsk in August of 1942. The pristine paint work is representative of the type. The upper wing insignia has been subdued leaving only the medium blue swastika with a thin white outline. (Ilmavoimat)

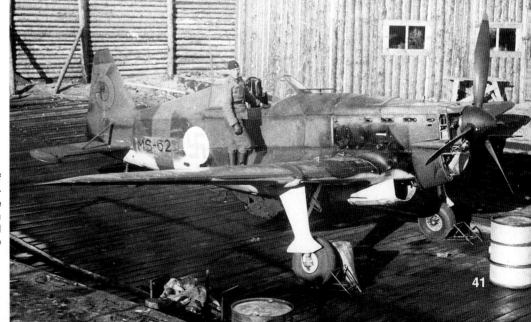

(Right) An MS 410 (MS-623) of *Lentolaivue* 28 undergoes minor maintenance at Hirvas in August of 1942. The 3rd Flight carried yellow tail numbers with a red border. This particular machine had a fixed liquid coolant radiator. (Eero Tiainen)

This captured Russian DB-3Ms served with the 2nd Flight of LeLv 48. DB-18 is seen at Luonetjärvi in August of 1942 wearing the flight's emblem, a black bear on a white patch. (Ilmavoimat)

(Above) Tupolev SBs were employed as submarine hunters by the 2nd Flight of *Lentolaivue* 6. The flight is lined up at Malmi for inspection on 23 September 1942. Standing in front of SB-1 (nearest the camera) is the flight leader, *Kapteeni* Birger Ek, a future Mannerheim Cross holder. (Ilmavoimat)

(Below) An SB-2M103A (SB-14) of 2/LeLv 6 is seen at Malmi on 3 October 1942. A bomb carrying duck served as the unit's emblem. From May of 1942 onward, captured aircraft were painted in a splinter type camouflage in black and olive green. (Ilmavoimat)

(Above) The State Aircraft Factory at Tampere was kept busy repairing captured aircraft throughout the war. IR-101, an I-16, was captured on 28 March 1942 during the invasion of Suursaari. Its use was limited to familiarization flights. Also under repair are an MS 406 (MS-302) and a Heinkel He 115 floatplane (HE-115) (SA-kuva)

In 1941 six Petlyakov Pe-2 bombers were purchased from Germany. Two more were captured later. The 1st Flight of LeLv 48 used the ex-Russian machines for bombing and reconnaissance missions. (Above right) PE-213 is seen at Utti in August of 1942, and (Below right) PE-212 visited Immola in July of 1942. (Pauli Ervi)

(Right) A pair of Tupolev SB bombers were converted to bomber crew trainers in early 1943 by adding a second cockpit in the navigator's position and covering the glazed nose with a wooden cone. SB-6, one of the converted trainers, is seen at Luonetjärvi in June of 1943 while serving with T-LeLv 17, the advanced training element of *Lentorykmentti* 4.

This 12-year old Ripon (RI-121) was relegated to courier duties. It was assigned to *Lentolaivue* 6 at Vesivehmaa in July of 1942. The fuselage bomb rack carries a cylindrical cargo container. (Olli Riekki)

Four obsolescent Dornier Do 22Kl float planes were purchased from Germany in 1941. The 1st Flight of *Lentolaivue* 6 used them as submarine hunters in the Gulf of Finland. DR-196, with a 200 kg depth charge mounted on the centerline, is moored at Santahamina off Helsinki in August of 1942. (Ilmavoimat)

Three Norwegian Hover M.F.11 float planes were interned in 1940 when they escaped the German invasion by flying to Finland. Later they were put into flying condition and the 4th Flight of LeLv 6 used them for maritime surveillance over the Baltic Sea. NK-172 carries a single depth charge while moored at Maarianhamina, Aaland in August of 1942.

Finland also interned a Norwegian Heinkel He 115A-2 float plane in 1940. Later refurbished as HE-115, it was assigned to *Lentolaivue* 46 and used to ferry commandos behind Russian lines. It is seen moored at Tiiksjärvi in July of 1942. (Pauli Ervi)

(Above) The six Junkers K 43fa light bombers purchased from Germany in 1930 proved to be very durable. JU-127 is tied up at the State Aircraft Factory mooring on lake Pyhäjärvi in May of 1943. Later serving in LeLv 44, JU-127 ferried commandos behind the Russian lines. (Aaretti Nieminen)

(Right) Five Russian Beriev MBR-2 flying boats were captured at the beginning of the Continuation War. MBR-2M34 (VV-182) of LeLv 15 is moored on lake Höytiäinen near Joensuu on 21 September 1941. All five aircraft were in poor condition and saw only limited service. (SA-kuva)

(Below) The old Blackburn Ripons continued to soldier on. RI-137 was issued to 1/LeLv 6 and flew anti-submarine patrols over the western Gulf of Finland. RI-137 is seen while moored at Santahamina off Helsinki in August of 1942. (Ilmavoimat)

(Above) CU-503, an ex-French Hawk 75, had the engine changed from a Wright Cyclone to a Pratt and Whitney Twin Wasp. The aircraft was parked at Nurmoila in August of 1942 while part of *Lentolaivue* 32. The aircraft carries a blue 3 with a white border on the rudder. (Aulis Bremer)

(Left) A Hawk 75A-2, CU-556/White 6, of *Lentolaivue* 32 stands in front of a service hanger at Nurmoila in July of 1942. The wing insignia has been reversed, an unusual practice at this late date. (Aulis Bremer)

(Below) Ex-Russian I-153 Chaikas of the 3rd Flight of LeLv 6 are lined up at Römpötti on 30 October 1942 after a reconnaissance mission over the eastern Gulf of Finland. The aircraft are numbered IT-15, IT-20, IT-19 and IT-18. The tail numbers are white. (Ilmavoimat)

(Above) Brewster B-239s of 2/LeLv 24 cruise above Tiiksjärvi in September of 1942. BW-352 was the mount of *Vääpeli* (Master Sergeant) Eero Kinnunen, an ace with 22.5 victories. His victory marks and the 2nd Flight emblem, a black farting elk, are carried on the tail. (Pauli Ervi)

(Right) FR-167 was a Fokker D.XXI fitted with locally designed retractable landing gear. It is at Vesivehmaa in October of 1943 while on strength with T-LeLv 35, an advanced training squadron. The fuselage guns fired along the outside of the engine cowling.

(Below) A Fokker C. X (FK-99) parked along side a pair of Fokker D.XXIs at the Immola depot on 25 May 1942. The C. X went to LeLv 16, while the closest D.XXI (FR-139) was assigned to T-LeLv 35.

The D.XXI has a white rudder, used by a number of training aircraft. (Pauli Ervi)

(Above) This winter camouflaged Morane MS-328 of 1/LeLv 28 was on loan to *Lentolaivue* 34 at Utti in March of 1943 for familiarization flights. It retains its earlier victory markings on the lower edge of the vertical fin. (Paavo Saari)

(Left) A Dornier Do 17Z (DN-64) of *Lentolaivue* 46 was photographed at Tiiksjärvi on 12 January 1943. It was flown by *Lentomestari* Viljo Salminen, the first Mannerheim Cross holder of the bomber arm. Now assigned to mapping duties, the unit's aircraft had playing cards painted on their noses. (SA-kuva)

(Below) The captured Tupolev SBs issued to *Lentolaivue* 6 were ordered to bomb Soviet airfields outside Leningrad in March of 1943. SB-13, wearing a scruffy coat of white camouflage on its upper surfaces, is parked at Immola during these missions. (Paavo Saari)

(Above) A Brewster B-239 (BW-364) of 3/LeLv 24 was flown by *Lentomestari* Ilmari Juutilainen. The aircraft is parked at Immola in May of 1943 and carries Juutilainen's full score of 36 victories, all of which were scored with the Brewster. The tail of BW-383, flown by *Lentomestari* Martti Alho (15 victories), is parked on the far side. (Tor Krause)

(Right) A Fiat G.50 (FA-19) was assigned to *Lentolaivue* 26 at Immola in October of 1943. This machine retains the 1938 model raised decking behind the cockpit. The two white horizontal bars on the rudder denoted the 2nd Flight. (Heimo Malmberg)

(Below) CU-505, a Hawk 75 of LeLv 32, warms up at Nurmoila in August of 1943. The revetments were built using local pine trees. The aircraft carries a blue 5 with a white border on the rudder. This machine was re-fitted with a Twin Wasp engine. (Aulis Bremer)

(Above) This Bf 109G-2 (MT-222) was the mount of ace Warrant Officer Ilmari Juutilainen while serving with the 1st Flight of *Lentolaivue* 34. The aircraft is parked at Helsinki-Malmi in May of 1943. Juutilainen was the top scorer in the Messerschmitt Bf 109, claiming 58 kills. His score eventually totaled 94 Soviet aircraft. (Andreas Donner)

(Left) The thirty Messerschmitt fighters purchased from Germany had just arrived. The commander of LeLv 34, *Majuri* Eino Luukkanen, stands in front of MT-203, a Bf 109G-2 at Utti in April of 1943. He accrued a total of 56 victories and won the Mannerheim Cross. (Paavo Saari)

(Below) A Bf 109G-2 (MT-215) of 1/LeLv 34 sits in the Malmi hanger in May of 1943. The tactical number, outlined in white on the cowl, was the last number of the serial. Red 5 was flown by *Ylikersantti* Eino Peltola, an ace with 10.5 victories. Germany agreed to cover the Bf 109 losses and within a year, Finland would receive a total of 48 Bf 109G-2 fighters. (Andreas Donner)

(Above) The duty pilots of 1/LeLv 34 wait at Utti on 1 June 1943. From left are *Luutnantti* Väinö Pokela, *Vääpeli* Mauno Fräntilä, *Lentomestari* Oiva Tuominen, *Luutnantti* Kalevi Tervo, *Ylikersantti* Gösta Lönnfors, and *Ylikersantti* Urho Lehto. The planes behind are MT-212, 222, 207, and 217. (ECPA)

(Right) 1/LeLv 34 pilot and Mannerheim Cross holder Warrant Officer Oiva Tuominen leans on his Messerschmitt MT-220, Red Zero, at Utti in June of 1943. Tuominen ultimately scored 44 victories. All of the Messerschmitts were camouflaged in the standard German gray scheme of RLM 74 *Graugrun* and RLM 75 *Grau Violett* over RLM 76 *Lichtblau*. (Paavo Saari)

The second ranking Finnish ace *Luutnantti* Hans Wind led the 3rd Flight of *Lentolaivue* 24. He stands in front of his aircraft, BW-393/Orange 9, at Suulajärvi on 12 September 1943. He scored 39 kills in the Brewster and another 36 while flying Messerschmitts, gaining a total of 75 confirmed victories. Wind was awarded the Mannerheim Cross in 1943, and the next year, became one of four Finnish soldiers to receive a second Mannerheim Cross. (SA-kuva)

(Above) The twenty-four Junkers Ju 88A-4 bombers purchased from Germany arrived in April of 1943. JK-265 was assigned to the 3rd Flight of *Lentolaivue* 44 and is parked at Onttola in June of 1943.

The fighter type tactical number on the tail was painted as a yellow outline.

(Above) JK-252 of 1/LeLv 44 is seen at Onttola in June of 1943. The tactical number two is a light blue-gray outline. The camouflage colors were the standard German greens RLM 70 *Schwarzgrun* and RLM 71 *Dunkelgrun* over lower surfaces of RLM 65 *Hellblau*.

(Below) In 1942 four Ilyushin Il-4 bombers were purchased from German stocks of captured war material and assigned to the 2nd Flight of LeLv 48. DF-23 is seen at Luonetjärvi in August of 1943. The aircraft is wearing a splinter camouflage scheme of olive green and black over light blue-gray. (Ilmavoimat)

(Above) Curtiss Hawks of *Lentolaivue* 32 cruise in an echelon formation over the River Svir on 16 October 1943. Closest to the camera is Yellow Zero (CU-580) piloted by *Luutnantti* Jaako Hillo (8 victories). To cover attrition, fifteen additional Curtiss Hawk 75As were purchased from Germany in 1943. (SA-kuva)

(Right) In 1942 thirty-two Morane-Saulnier MS 406 fighters were purchased from Germany to equip an additional squadron. MS-605 of the 1/LeLv 14 has just returned to Tiiksjärvi from a sortie in May of 1943. (Elias Järvineva)

(Below) A Junkers Ju 88 (JK-262) is bombed up at Onttola in June of 1943. Red 3, assigned to the 2nd Flight of *Lentolaivue* 44, had red spinner tips. Small tractors pulled sledges due to the lack of proper bomb trolleys.

The Continuation War - Early 1944

The last year of the Continuation War against the Soviet Union started out quietly. By the end of January however, the Russians suddenly broke the siege of Leningrad. In the eyes of the Finns, this changed the military-political situation overnight. To boost negotiations for a separate peace, Soviet long-range bombers began attacking Helsinki, the Finnish capital, carrying out large raids on three separate nights during February. To counter the attacks, Finnish bombers joined the returning Russian formations and released bombs on the well-lit airfields, destroying parked and landing aircraft. Especially destructive was the late evening of 9 March 1944, when the Finns destroyed at least ten Russian bombers with many others damaged and gasoline reserves destroyed.

During the winter of 1944, the Finnish Air Force went through a

Finland purchased 112 Messerschmitt Bf 109G-6 fighters and two Bf 109G-8 reconnaissance fighters from Germany in 1944. MT-483, a Bf 109G-8, sits in a revetment at Lappeenranta in July of 1944. It was flown by the 1st Flight leader of *Hävittäjälentolaivue* 24 (HLeLv 24), Captain Atte Lassila. (Jaakko Hyvönen)

minor reorganization which resulted in new names for the flying units. The new names specifically identified the role of the squadrons as *Hävittäjälentolaivue* (HLeLv) for fighter squadrons, *Pommituslentolaivue* (PLeLv) for bomber squadrons, and *Tiedustelulentolaivue* (TLeLv) for reconnaissance squadrons.

As the air war again began to escalate, the Finnish bomber force began to reestablish itself. On the evening of 3 April 1944 thirty-four bombers attacked Kähy airfield near Leningrad destroying 17 out of 57 Russian aircraft on the ground.

On 17 May 1944, a formation of 27 Soviet bombers escorted by 15 fighters arrived to bomb Kotka, the northern supply point of the mine-belt. Eleven Bf 109s scrambled and attacked from below shooting down eight bombers and three fighters.

On 14 February 1944 all unit names were altered, to indicate their role as a fighter, bomber or reconnaissance squadron. The abbreviations were HLeLv (fighter), PLeLv (bomber), and TLeLv (reconnaissance). A Bf 109G-2 (MT-213) of 2/HLeLv 24 sits between missions at

Suulajärvi in May of 1944. In the foreground with a walking stick is the squadron commander *Majuri* Jorma Karhunen, a Mannerheim-Cross holder and an ace with 31 victories.

(Above) In 1943 the factory built 30 short nose Blenheim IIs and ten long nosed Blenheim IVs in 1944. One of the latter (BL-196) of 2/*Pommituslentolaivue* 42 (PLeLv 42) is parked at Immola in April of 1944. (Paavo Saari)

(Right) In 1944 five obsolete Junkers W 34hi aircraft were purchased from Germany for telegraphist training. JU-132 of the Communications School is seen at Taipalsaari in July of 1944.

(Below) A battle worn Brewster B-239 (BW-374) rests at Suulajärvi on 8 May 1944 just before its transfer from HLeLv 24 to HLeLv 26. The aircraft was assigned to *Luutnantti* Eero Riihikallio of the 2nd Flight. Riihikallio scored 16.5 kills before the war in Europe ended one year later. (SA-kuva)

The VL Myrsky (Storm) was designed and built by the State Aircraft Factory. MY-5 was the first of 51 series built fighters and is parked at the factory in May of 1944. In January of 1944 a directive was issued changing the white disk of the national insignia to RLM 65 Hellblau. The change was applicable to all new aircraft and those coming from a major repair. (VL)

The Great Offensive

In June of 1944 the Soviet Union launched its fourth major offensive of the war. The Russians attacked German forces along the entire eastern front, from the Baltic Sea to the Balkans. On 9 June 1944, the Red Army on the Finnish Front joined in the attack when fifteen divisions, covered by 1550 aircraft, surged over the Karelian Isthmus. To repel the attack, the Finns had two divisions at the spearhead supported by 30 fighters and 60 bombers. Under such pressure, the Finns retreated to Viipuri which, in turn, was lost on 20 June. That same day, the Russians launched an offensive on the Onletets Isthmus north of Lake Onega and drove west. The Russians launched a third offensive on the isthmus between Lake Onega and Lake Ladoga on 21 June 1944.

Finnish aircraft flew several missions daily and conducted operations during the light Nordic nights, often engaging 200-plus strong Soviet formations. Finnish fighters scored numerous kills well out of proportion to their own small numbers, while the bombers caused havoc among the densely packed Soviet troop, tank, and artillery columns. During the concentrated Finnish bombing attacks on the Karelian Isthmus, the average number of bombers was 35 and the escort was usually 16 Messerschmitts. The escort was so effective that not a single bomber was lost to Russian fighters. Nevertheless, such successes were merely pinpricks against the growing Soviet forces.

To assist Finland, Detachment *"Kuhlmey"* came from the German front with 30 Focke Wulf Fw 190A-6 fighters and Fw 190F-8 fighter-bombers, and 25 Junkers Ju 87D-5 dive-bombers. The Finnish fighter units received 80 new Messerschmitt Bf 109G-6s for defense. While their performance was remarkable, their numbers were insufficient to stem the Russian onslaught.

Despite Russian progress on the ground, the Finns were able to stop the drives by 12 July 1944 when the Soviet high command slowed the attacks and transferred the bulk of their troops southward to the German front. The Allied invasion of Normandy was now a month old and the Soviets did not wish to be late in their run to Berlin. During the 38 day offensive, the bombers of LeR 4 had flown 1,232 sorties on 36 missions and the fighters of LeR 3 another 2,168 sorties on 355 missions.

Throughout the war, the Finnish government had continued to act as a co-belligerent with Germany against the USSR. The overall situation now permitted — perhaps required — a separate peace with the Soviet Union. When Marshall Mannerheim became President in August of 1944, the Finns initiated efforts to reach a peace settlement with the Soviets. Above all, President Mannerheim wanted Finland out of the war with her sovereignty intact. A truce was signed on 4 September 1944 with a provisional peace treaty following on 19 September. The treaty reaffirmed the earlier Treaty of Moscow that had ended the Winter War in 1940 and established new borders between Finland and the USSR.

During 1944, Finnish fighters had shot down 578 Soviet aircraft and the anti-aircraft units had accounted for another 543 planes. Operational losses were 73 aircraft. Finnish front-line strength stood at 198 serviceable aircraft when hostilities ended.

Hävittäjälentolaivue 26 flew Brewsters during the final stages of the war. The engine of BW-384, White 7, is being started with a hand crank at Immola on 15 June 1944. The location of the tactical number identified the 1st Flight of LeR 3 fighter squadrons since 22 May 1944. (SA-kuva)

(Above) JK-268 of 3/PLeLv 44 returns from a mission to the Karelian Isthmus on 14 June 1944. The aircraft is piloted by Mannerheim Cross holder *Lentomestari* Unto Oksala. The aircraft wears a typical 1944 camouflage of olive green and black upper surfaces over light blue-gray under surfaces. The 'Eastern Front' markings, spinner tips, and tail number are yellow. (SA-kuva)

(Below) The workshops at Immola were constantly busy repairing minor combat and training damage. The aircraft here represent a typical day on 15 June 1944. The aircraft clockwise are a Ju 88 (JK-254), Blenheim (BL-197), Ju 88 (JK-265), Viima (VI-2), and a Brewster B-239 (BW-375). (SA-kuva)

(Above) A Bf 109G-6 (MT-416) of 3/HLeLv 34, lands at Taipalsaari in June of 1944. There is a yellow 6 on the fin. The number's position on the fin identified the 3rd Flight. *Ylikersantti* Aaro Nuorala, a 14.5 victory ace, was one of the pilots flying this aircraft. (Kauko Risku)

(Below) This Bf 109G-6 (MT-423) of 1/HLeLv 34 was the mount of Staff Sergeant Hemmo Leino (11 victories). The aircraft is parked at Kymi in June of 1944 carrying the official squadron emblem, a stylized fledgling eagle on the rudder. This machine also has the tall fin and rudder of late production G-6s (Tor Krause)

(Below) In December of 1943, the Finns captured a single Russian Curtiss P-40M-1-CU Warhawk. It was refurbished and delivered to HLeLv 32 for familiarization flights. KH-51, wearing a patchy coat of olive green, was photographed at Mensuvaara in August of 1944.

58

(Above) Bf 109G-6/R6 (MT-453) was parked at Taipalsaari in July of 1944. The aircraft is equipped with the underwing 20mm cannon packs. This Messerschmitt was often flown by *Vääpeli* Antti Tani (21.5 victories) of 1/HLeLv 34. (Kauko Tuomikoski)

(Below) 3/HLeLv 24 aircraft (MT-441/Yellow 1 and MT-476/Yellow 7) stand ready for a mission at Lappeenranta on 3 July 1944. The former was flown by *Luutnantti* Ahti Laitinen with 12 victories and the latter by Mannerheim Cross holder *Vääpeli* Nils Katajainen with 35.5 victories. (SA-kuva)

(Below) Three Lavochkin LaGG-3 aircraft were captured in 1942 and later repaired at the State Aircraft Factory. They were issued to *Hävittäjälentolaivue* 32. LG-3 is seen at Mensuvaara in July of 1944.

The upper part of the yellow nose band was over painted on all aircraft on 13 June 1944.

(Above) This Junkers Ju 87D-5 (S7+JH) of 1./SG 3 at Immola was flown by *Feldwebel* Oswald Gado on 2 July 1944. (SA-kuva).

To assist Finland during the Soviet's so-called "great offensive", *Gefechtsverband* (Detachment) Kuhlmey arrived at Immola on 16 June 1944 with 80 aircraft. The unit consisted of I/SG 3, 4 and 5/JG 54, and 1/SG 5. Detachment Kuhlmey flew combat missions over the Karelian Isthmus for five weeks.

(Left) A Focke Wulf Fw 190F-8, Black 10, of 1./SG 5 is parked at Immola on 28 June 1944. It was piloted by *Feldwebel* Hartmut Gellwart (SA-kuva).

(Below) White 20, an Fw 190A-6 of 4./JG 54, is serviced between sorties at Immola on 2 July 1944. (SA-kuva).

(Above) JK-260 of the 2nd Flight of *Pommituslentolaivue* 44 prepares for take off from Onttola for a mission on 30 June 1944. Intense operations have left the plane wearing the 1st Flight colors, a light blue-gray number 4 on the fin. The aircraft also wears toned down national insignia. (SA-kuva)

(Below) Ju 88s of PLeLv 44 taxi out for the same mission from Onttola on 30 June 1944. JK-268 in the foreground was assigned to the 3rd Flight. JK-256, flown by the 1st Flight leader *Kapteeni* Erkki Itävuori, is next; this plane has a light blue-gray outlined number 1 on the fin. The last aircraft, JK-252, was attached to the 1st Flight. (SA-kuva)

The Lapland War

According to the conditions of the new treaty with the Soviets, German troops in northern Finland had to be pushed out of the country. With assistance from the Finns, the Russians began an offensive in the north to clear out the Germans. By the end of October, nearly all German troops had been pushed into Norway. Since German aircraft were seldom encountered, the fighters made only three claims. However, accurate German anti-aircraft guns took a toll of eleven Finnish aircraft. Under the primitive conditions in the arctic winter weather, the Finnish Air Force suffered the loss of another six planes.

In two wars against the Soviet Union, Finland had fought and preserved her independence. Finnish forces destroyed 3,313 Soviet aircraft, the flying units claiming 1,807 and the anti-aircraft artillery 1,345, with the rest being shared by naval units, observed crashes, or were destroyed on the ground. The Finnish Air Force lost 257 aircraft on operations and another 215 due to non-operational reasons. An additional 100 aircraft were destroyed in training accidents. Personnel losses amounted to 353 airmen killed or missing in action and another 86 lost in flying accidents.

Brewsters of HLeLv 26 were used for reconnaissance against the Germans in Lapland. BW-355/Yellow 1 takes off from Onttola to Vaala on 2 October 1944. The inscription NOKA below the wind-

Lentorykmentti **4 was used against the Germans in Lapland. JK-266 of PLeLv 44 waits for its bomb load at Kemi in October of 1944 just before the first snowfall. The yellow Eastern Front markings were now painted over. The fin has a yellow outlined number 1.**

The Lapland War - Camouflage and Markings

The peace treaty signed with the Soviet Union in September of 1944 resulted in Finnish military operations against the Germans in northern Finland. The camouflage schemes remained the same, however, there were two fundamental changes in markings. First, the Finnish Air Force (FAF) removed the German required yellow 'Eastern Front' markings from the cowls, lower wing tips, and aft fuselages of all of their aircraft. Second, the FAF replaced their historic *Hakaristi* insignia with a roundel in the Finnish national colors of white, blue, and white. The insignia change was made permanent on 1 April 1945 due to pressure from the victorious Allies. As far as the Allies were concerned, the swastika, regardless of its color, orientation, or historical significance to Finland, was not welcome in the skies over Europe.

screen stands for the donor (Nokia Oy) of the funds used to purchase this particular aircraft. (Carl-Erik Bruun)

Tiedustelulentolaivue (TLeLv) 12 was one of two squadrons equipped with the VL Myrsky. Yellow Zero (MY-20) of the 2nd Flight is parked at Joroinen after the end of the Continuation War in September of 1944. The Myrsky was the only Finnish-designed fighter to see service. Although a pleasant aircraft to fly, it went through a protracted development period with a number of aircraft suffering inflight structural failures. Additionally, the wooden wings and steel tubing fuselage structure did not fare well in the Arctic weather.

(Right) 2/TLeLv 12 was subordinated to HLeLv 26 in the Lapland War. Yellow 6 (MY-16) runs up its engine at Kemi on 24 October 1944. The white lightning bolt on the cowling is the flight emblem.

(Below) During 1944 and 1945 VL fitted all the remaining Morane-Saulnier MS 406 fighter aircraft with captured Russian Klimov M-105P engines. The 1100 horsepower engine considerably improved performance. The re-engined aircraft were known as Mörkö Moranes. MSv-633 is parked at Rissala in March of 1945 while attached to Hävittäjälentolaivue 21. The unit, renumbered on 4 December 1944, was formerly designated HLeLv 28. (Aulis Bremer)

Appendices

GLOSSARY

Finnish	Abbreviation	English
Flygflottilj (Swedish)	F	Flying Wing
Hävittäjälentolaivue	HLeLv	Fighter Squadron
Ilmailukoulu	Ilm.K.	Aviation School
Lentolaivue	LLv, LeLv	Flying Squadron
Lentoasema	L.As.	Flying Station
Lentorykmentti	LeR	Flying Regiment
Lentosotakoulu	LeSK	Air Fighting School
Pommituslentolaivue	PLeLv	Bomber Squadron
Täydennyslentolaivue	T-LeLv	Advanced Training Sqdn
Tiedustelulentolaivue	TLeLv	Reconnaissance Sqdn
Valtion Lentokonetehdas	VL	State Aircraft Factory

RANKS

Finnish	US	Abbreviation
Kersantti	Sergeant	Sgt
Ylikersantti	Staff Sergeant	SSgt
Vääpeli	Master Sergeant	MSgt
Lentomestari	Warrant Officer	W/O
Vänrikki	Second Lieutenant	2nd Lt
Luutnantti	Lieutenant	Lt
Kapteeni	Captain	Capt
Majuri	Major	Maj
Everstiluutnantti	Lieutenant Colonel	Lt Col
Eversti	Colonel	Col

AIRCRAFT TYPES

Code	Acquired	Serials	Type	Code	Acquired	Serials	Type
BL	97	104-190, 196-205	Bristol Blenheim I, II and IV	JU	12	120,122-128, 131-135	Junkers K 43 and W 34
BU	19	59-75, 214, 216	Bristol Bulldog IVA	LY	12	114-125	Westland Lysander I
BW	44	351-394	Brewster Model 239	MS	87	301-330, 601-657	Morane-Saulnier M.S. 406
CU	44	501-507, 551-587	Curtiss Hawk 75A	MT	162	201-248, 401-514	Messerschmitt Bf 109G
DB	11	11-21	Ilyushin DBM-3M	MY	51	1-51	VL Myrsky II
DN	15	51-65	Dornier Do 17Z	PE	8	211-217, 301	Petlyakov Pe-2
FA	35	1-35	Fiat G.50	PY	41	1-41	VL Pyry
FK	39	78-111, 111-115	Fokker C.X	RI	26	121, 129-143, 150-159	Blackburn Ripon IIF
FO	19	39, 65-77, 19, 23, 80, 65, 66	Fokker C.V	SB	24	1-24	Tupolev SB
FR	97	76-167, 171-175	Fokker D.XXI	SM	39	127-165	Letov S 218A
GL	30	251-280	Gloster Gladiator II	SZ	35	1-35	Focke Wulf Fw 44J
HC	13	451-462, 465	Hawker Hurricane I	TU	31	149-179	VL Tuisku
IT	22	11-31	Polikarpov I-153	VI	24	1-23, 40	VL Viima
JK	24	251-274	Junkers Ju 88A-4				

MOST SUCCESSFUL AIRMEN

FIGHTER PILOTS

Rank	Name	Unit(s)	Sorties	Victories	Mannerheim-Cross
W/O	E. Ilmari Juutilainen	24, 34	437	94	26.4.42, 28.6.44
Capt	Hans H. Wind	24	302	75	31.7.43, 28.6.44
Maj	Eino A. Luukkanen	24, 30, 34	441	56	18.6.44
W/O	Urho S. Lehtovaara	28, 34	400 +	44.5	9.7.44
W/O	Oiva E. Tuominen	26, 30, 34	400 +	44	17.8.41
Capt	R. Olli Puhakka	26, 34	401	42	21.12.44
Lt	Olavi K. Puro	30, 24	207	36	
SSgt	Nils E. Katajainen	24	196	35.5	21.12.44
Lt	Lauri V. Nissinen	24	300 +	32.5	5.7.42
Lt	Kyösti K. Karhila	32, 34, 24	304	32	
Capt	Jorma Karhunen	24	350 +	31	8.9.42
Sgt	Emil O. Vesa	24	198	29.5	
Sgt	T. Tapio Järvi	24	247	28.5	
MSgt	Klaus J. Alakoski	26, 34	239	26	
Lt	A. Kalevi Tervo	24, 32, 34	150 +	23	
Lt	Jorma K. Saarinen	24	139	23	
W/O	Eero A. Kinnunen	24	300 +	22.5	
SSgt	Antti J. Tani	28, 34	272	21.5	
Lt	U. Paavo Myllylä	28, 34	420	21	
Maj	Veikko J. Karu	26, 28, 30	400 +	10	6.11.42
Col	Gustaf Erik Magnusson	24, LeR 3	158	5.5	26.6.44

OTHER AIRCREW

Rank	Name	Unit(s)	Sorties	Mannerheim-Cross
W/O	Viljo F. Salminen	44, 46	200 +	5.11.41 as bomber pilot
Capt	Paavo E. Kahla	14, 16, 26	250 +	26.4.42 as navigator
Lt	Rolf R. Winqvist	46, 44	150 +	26.4.42 as navigator
Maj	Auvo H. Maunula	12, 28	200 +	8.9.42 as recce pilot
Capt	R. Birger Ek	44, 6	200 +	8.3.43 as anti-sub pilot
W/O	Unto J. Oksala	44	150 +	21.11.43 as bomber pilot
Capt	Tauno V. Iisalo	44	127	21.12.44 as bomber pilot
Lt	Lauri A. Äijö	44, 48	110	21.12.44 as navigator